Editor in Chief
Harry Lake

Editors at Large
Joe Andrews
Pete Martin

Copy Editors
Nick Burt
Ben Brown
John Childs
Martin Dreneau

Design
Scott McRoy
Richard Harries

Photography
James Hendley, Nathan Congleton
Amy Maidment, Robbie Jay Barratt
Jon Roberts, Andy Ford,
Mehdi Lacoste, Chad Gibson

Illustrators
Mago Dovjenko, Steve Welsh (Miniboro),
Jorge Lawerta, ilovedust, Golden Wolf,
Conal Deeney

Special Thanks
Julian Stone, Paolo Hewitt, Andy Walsh,
Andy Walker, Matt Dent, Chris Dent,
Hovig Yardim, Luke Zak, James Pleass,
Clement Lacour, Sarah Stade, NYCFC
Christian Pflug, Terence Parris,
Carsten Cramer, Jens Volke, Frank Gräfen,
Jenny Simmons, Ben Goldhagen,
Mark Graham, Joe Carby, Gary Aspden,
Florence Garlaza, Christian Stadil,
Gareth Kerr, Ant Baena, Eddy Jennings,
and Winston Agogo.

To Advertise
advertising@soccerbible.com

Printed By
Four Way Print Ltd

Distributed by
www.marketforce.co.uk

Contact Us
u2us@soccerbible.com

DISCLAIMER:

SOCCERBIBLE

MAVERICKS & DISRUPTORS

—

In a game that is ruled by such fine margins, it is often
a spark that lights the fuse. A match of untamed tendencies,
this issue is dedicated to those wildcards that defy the rules
of convention while adding a dash of danger to the delivery.
The charming gods to the irritable sods, sliding close to
the line in delivering that perfectly weighted pass.
We hope you enjoy.

CONTENTS
—

ASICS TIGER

WINTER TRAIL

COLLECTION

@runwiththegoldenwolf

MAN.MYTH. LEGEND.

—

Robin Friday as told by Paolo Hewitt

Photography by James Hendley

Nevermind scruff of the neck; Robin Friday took the ball at his feet, the pints at the bar and his life in whatever lane suited him there and then. Paolo Hewitt gives us an introduction to a lasting legacy of a legend.

CHARLIE:

Ok Robin, I'm going to put you
in the team on Sunday.

ROBIN:

Boss that is fucking great,
I'll tell you what, I won't
drink, I won't go with any
women and I won't get in
any fights.

CHARLIE:

Robin, you can lie to me once,
but not three times.

Unleashing those ramshackle creators of chaos in the shape of 'Mavericks and Disruptors', there was one story above all that provided inspiration that would underpin this issue. Wild, majestic, ferocious but never forgotten – the almost myth-like tale of Robin Friday.

THE true rock and roll rogue of football, his unrivalled story has been told from all senses: tactile in your touch, visible for your mind and sound for the soul. Like putting a still ball in the top corner with the outside of your foot, his spirit bigger than any form of media, this is a player, or more importantly a person, who could never be tamed, bottled or sold.

'The Man Don't Give a Fuck' and 'The Greatest Footballer You Never Saw' are just two ways in which the story of Robin Friday has been presented to the masses. The poetic form of film is next up, as a movie begins to depict this player of untamable type. Having got to know his family, friends, managers and fellow players, Paolo Hewitt quite literally co-wrote the book on Robin Friday with former Oasis bassist Paul McGuigan. We caught up with Paolo to get his unique take on Robin and help paint the picture of what made Reading Football Club's Player of the Millennium just so remarkable.

Paolo sets the scene. "Robin joined Reading in January 1974 and left in January '76. He walked out of football in April 1977." As turbulent as they come, it was a career of his own making. Going from borstal to labourer and then onto football player, it was instinctive, rebellious and raucous. Propping up the table, Reading plucked Robin from non-league Hayes. His reaction after scoring on his debut typified his effortless style and natural charisma. "I was thinking about back heeling the ball into the net but thought, I better not as it's your debut. Better not be too flashy."

Having got to know Robin in depth, the adventure of Paolo in uncovering this under-the-radar icon is well worthy of a story in itself. "That discovery, then meeting his wife, his brother, his friends and Charlie Hurley (the Reading manager who signed Robin), it was fantastic. In one way I spent such a lot of time with Robin. The great thing about it is, if I said I'm going to go and make a film about George Best, you already know that plot. Coming over on the ferry, Sir Matt Busby, European Cups. You know that story. Whereas with Robin, it's only the people in Reading and the people in Cardiff that know about him."

On and off the pitch he wrote his own rules. Wherever you look there is one goal that follows the name of Robin Friday around. "Clive Thomas, the referee, said the goal he scored against Tranmere Rovers was the best goal he had ever seen throughout his whole career." In telling the story, it's the blur of the lines that elevate the mystery, the magic. "I must have spoken to about fifty people about that goal. Some say it came from a throw-in, others a free kick. There's some myth about it. As long as you capture the truth and the sentiment of what this character was about, it doesn't really matter."

"He was one of these guys, for me anyway, it was like Wayne Rooney when he burst on the scene and he was playing football like he was still on the park. That's what Robin was. Everybody loves players like that, there's no artifice about them. They just love playing the game of football. Whether there was two people watching or twenty thousand, it didn't matter to them. That's what I really liked about Robin. He would go and kiss a policeman after scoring a goal or deck somebody or whatever."

The sentiment is what is most inspiring here. Restless, inquisitive, unmarkable mayhem, it wasn't just on the pitch that gave Robin his aura. An aura that Paolo says is truly unique, incomparable to anyone in today's game. "There's no one like Robin. There's obvious candidates but as we put in the book, if George (Best) was the first football pop star then Robin was the first rock star. He was total rock and roll. He even looked it. I haven't come across another player that would pick up a swan and let it loose in a bar somewhere."

Paolo draws comparisons with the engineered athletes of today's professional game. "If you go on holiday and come back a pound overweight, you'd probably get fined — this man got banned from the local pub ten times."

Not taming, rather guiding, Charlie Hurley is someone Paolo credits as getting the very best out of Robin. A relationship equally unique – more Pete and Carl than George and Ringo – it's rock and roll. In football terms, "Venables and Gazza, Busby and Best, it was like father and son."

Charlie clearly understood the kind of player he was dealing with, as Paolo explains. "When Charlie told Robin he is going to give him his debut, they were playing on a Sunday and he goes "Ok Robin, I'm going to put you in the team on Sunday" and Robin replies something like "Boss that is fucking great, I'll tell you what, I won't drink, I won't go with any women and I won't get in any fights" and Charlie goes "Robin, you can lie to me once, not three times".

"If you go on holiday and come back a pound overweight, you'd get fined...This man got banned from the local pub ten times."

"Knowing that he's got this talent but also knowing that he can't restrict that talent. He's got to let that talent go where it's going to go. I asked Charlie if he had any tactics with Robin and he said "Yeah, (just) give the ball to him". It worked out to be good tactics, they got promoted in the end."

A true character of the game, one of the reasons it has become a global language is because of the undertones of atmosphere that people like Robin Friday exuberate. "When he was at his peak Sheffield United offered 100 grand for him. Crazy money back then." His on the pitch value through the roof, the story is victorious yet sprinkled with pain and tragedy. In describing his aspirations for the upcoming biopic, Paolo explains, "The film has got to be like Robin. It's got to be sharp and sexy and funny and humorous and tragic. It's got to be everything he was. That's what it's got to be. In a sense, it's about a man and his demons."

A football career that ended when he wanted it to and a life well and truly lived, the story of Robin Friday is a perspective offering a humble triumph of football. An inspiration for this issue and for playing the game with flair, "his brother once said a really great thing to me 'you either have a giggle or die' and that was Robin, he had a giggle and he took that all the way through." There's only one Robin Friday.

EVOSPEED SL

MEET PUMA'S LIGHTEST MATCH BOOT EVER.

AVAILABLE NOW AT WWW.PRODIRECTSOCCER.COM

SWFC

—

Soho Warriors

Photography by Amy Maidment &
James Hendley

With nothing but dedication to the world of football, we head from the pitch to the pub with Soho Warriors as they look to pop their heads above the surface whilst taking on the underground.

When looking for creative inspiration, football is a place well dressed. Across all areas of the spectrum, from illustration to photography and every stopping point in between, there is a wealth of food for thought. One group that combines creativity and football in a truly unique fashion is the band of brothers at Soho Warriors.

Creators Matt and Chris Dent have gone from football-playing pioneers to agency advocates, turning their football team of likeminded individuals into a collective of collaboration, leading the charge as they champion creativity on and off the pitch.

The game on the pitch was very much their starting point. Inspired by New York-based Chinatown Soccer Club, which sees players from creative industries meet and play regularly, it was in 2010 that these creatives in their own right set out to bring together a group that shared similar interests, this time in London.

"We thought it could be interesting to see if we could find 20 or so like minded creatives who found themselves in a similar position to us, from the beginning it's been as much about collaborating as a group off the pitch as it has been about playing. I don't think initially we thought about the team as a brand, that side of things has developed over time."

Above 'The Albion
In Goldsmith's Row'.
An inspiration for
the appreciator of
glorious memorabilia.

SWFC. Curating a
community inspired
by creative football.
Going for the win on
and off the pitch.

Nostalgia-fuelled football passion. Imagine Football Manager – you have the joy of being the all-round architect of your game: you're the manager, the marketing chief, the kit creator, the event manager and the player. What's more, it's all housed under the mutual appreciation of beautiful football that the design world offers. 'Soho Warriors' has become a brand in itself, and as well as merchandise on show, it is 'SWFC' the agency that five years down the line is starting to flourish.

From the early days, Matt and Chris were knocking on the doors of brands in the hope of sharing their vision, something a little easier said than done. "We went to adidas early on to explain who we are and what we were planning to do, it's fair to say we had a few confused looks during that meeting. It's been a difficult sell at times as its a new concept but adidas have shown a great understanding and interest in what we are trying to do from that very first chat four years ago."

Backed up with a strategy and long term aspirations, their ideals have been bought into and, trusting their creative nuances, it's most recently that collaborations have proved the pudding is of appreciative and innovative tastes. Having hosted the London

instalment of the adidas 'FANATIC' tournament, along with an appetiser for a feast of football culture in the shape of the 'adidas Clubhouse', SWFC now has two incredibly well-rounded events under its belt (the latter largely inspired by The Albion on Goldsmith's Row) and the eye-line moves further down the line – that perfect threaded pass to the next project.

Having the luxury of carefully choosing projects, they pride themselves on making that killer pass. In the way that a perfect touch is often more heroic than a scuffed-in finish, it's the beauty of the game that will underline their choices over the glamour of the brightest boot launch. In this case we have faith that the perfect touch would still be finished by a volley into the top corner. Not looking to grab the headlines, the next phase in the journey is to "build a community" and "celebrate the finer details of football". An exciting next chapter awaits, and all the while, football on the pitch on a Tuesday and Friday evening will reign supreme.

With the company registered and ready to go, it's the wider football world in which they look to progress, now with a breadth of talents to call upon from the team. Amateur players on the pitch though professionals of the highest order off it is where they find themselves. An infectious passion for the game and a community of appreciation, they've cut themselves apart creatively and we're proud to call them mates. sohowarriorsfc.com

KEEP RIGHT

—

Underground F.C.

Photography by Chad Gibson LOCALFC

Raw, enigmatic, intoxicating. Underground Football Club is a spectacle of creative football culture brought to life on the small sided court. Anchored in an abandoned workshop located in Saint-Ouen, Paris – a location of raw beauty – this summer's final pulled in 1,500 likeminded folk from creative industries across Europe who vied for supremacy inside huge, octagonal metallic cages.

A sound of football from the underground, the event brought together a mixture of teams including fashion label Kitsuné, Italian magazine Toilet Paper, and London's very own Soho Warriors. This was a breeding ground for ideas and collaboration as much as a celebration of the world's greatest language. We spoke to the creator of Underground Football Club, Victor Coeur, to find out how this movement began.

For anybody new to Underground Football Club, can you introduce the concept?

Underground Football Club is a tournament dedicated to creative people, creative players and creative guests. So the teams who are playing tonight, they all come from creative universes – they come from fashion, design, music, they are DJs, artists, illustrators. We are trying to bring all of these people together to make a special connection. I think events like these help the creative culture that's building within football. It helps us to show something different and show that football is not only about television but is also in the blood of creative people. Tonight we're offering an experience to the players and to the guests.

Retro inspired adidas jersey worn by Soho Warriors goalkeeper, Chris Dent.

Creator of Underground Football Club, Victor Coeur.

Where was the idea born from?

I was living in New York three years ago and I heard about these Chinatown clandestine parties with amateur boxing matches. Everybody was talking about it, everyone wanted to go, but it was impossible to find it – there was no information, no address, nothing. In the US, football still isn't as big as it is in Europe, so I thought we should take the idea and bring it to Paris, but with football. I called my friend Rod Reynolds, the founder of Dcontract (the agency behind Underground Football Club) and with this idea we developed Underground Football Club.

Can you talk to us about your partnership with adidas and their involvement in the project?

When we created the concept we presented it to brands including adidas and Nike. Immediately adidas were as excited as we were to make it happen. They really love football – not only professional football you see in super expensive stadiums, but also football from the streets. They backed the whole project from the start and have been a huge part in making this season's tournament a success – as you can see, all of the players here are wearing the new adidas football shoes. It's a special relationship between ourselves and adidas and they are helping us to build this project because we are creating a unique experience for people.

What teams do you have involved in the tournament?

We try to have teams who are not really playing football every day. In each country we try to identify who are the most creative people and the people who are the best in their fields. Tonight we have six French teams and four foreign teams – for next year's final we would like to do five teams from Paris and five teams from five different countries, but we would like each team from each country to come from their own local competition. This year we had a competition in Paris where teams would play for a place in tonight's final. We would like to do a one-day tournament in cities like Berlin, London, Barcelona and Milan, where the best teams would come to Paris for the big final.

How much work goes on behind the scenes to pull off an event like this?

So much! At the agency we have three people working on this every day and we have been working on the event for the last six months. There's also the work

Records Collection FC circle for a pre-match huddle.

that goes into the location, the set-up, the lights, the security, the guests and the DJs. We are starting from zero; we don't have our own football arena for example. So it's pretty hard, but it's very exciting and we love it. This is our job, to create a new atmosphere and something that's special for one night only.

What was the reaction like following last year's tournament?

It was amazing because we received a ton of emails from people who wanted to play, but unfortunately we can't say yes to everyone. We realised that there are other people like us in France and also across Europe who like football, but maybe in a different way. We created something in France that connected us to people in other countries. We are a small community, but we have the same ambitions and like the same things.

How have things changed from season one?

This year we have two pitches and a big stage where 'La Femme' and 'Made in Taiwan' will play later. So we've really reached the next level with this year's tournament, but we don't want to stop there. We are already looking ahead to next year and doing even bigger things. My dream would be to have a tower of football cages one on top of each other where teams could play!

An investment into a pure side of the game, Underground Football Club is a type of football totally removed from the mainstream and an event that must be experienced. From the first whistle to the curtain call, the event came, saw and utterly conquered, leaving Paris high on the spirit of this diverse football culture. We'll be back next year.

Champions of Underground Football Club 2015,
Records Collection FC.

P. BATTISTON - DENTAL RECORD FORM

IDENTIFICATION NO: FRA-03

EXAMINER: H Schumacher

DATE: 08 JULY 1982

RESTORATIONS & MISSING TEETH

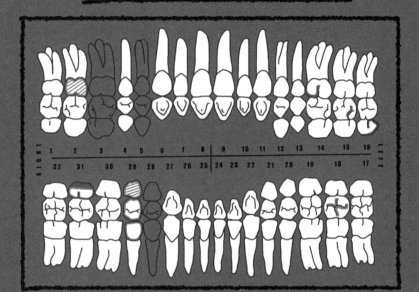

SYMBOLS AND CHARTING:

#3 impacted & missing

#5 impacted & missing

#28 impacted & missing

EST AGE: 25
SEX: Male
RACE: Cauc

DISEASES AND ABNORMALITIES

REMARKS:

If thats all thats wrong with him — I will pay him the crowns

HOSPITAL REPORT: three broken ribs / cracked vertabra

@miniboro

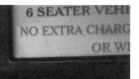

6 SEATER VEHI
NO EXTRA CHARG
OR WI

SITTIN' HERE THINKIN'

—

Joey Barton

Photography by Robbie Jay Barrett

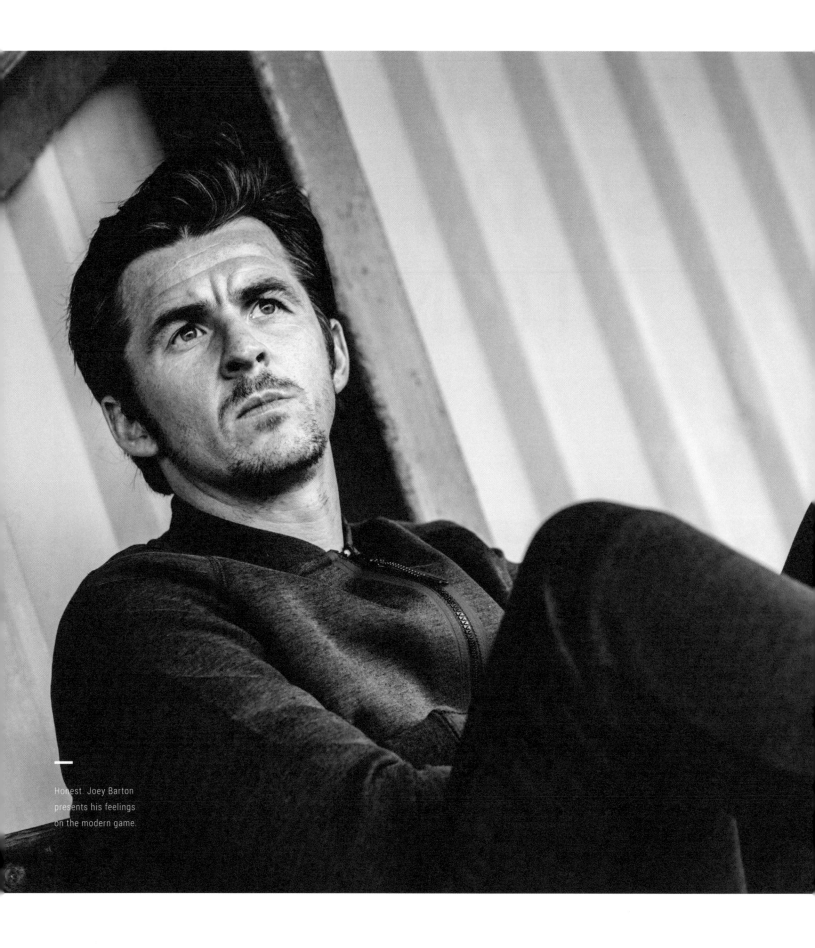

Honest. Joey Barton
presents his feelings
on the modern game.

Joey Barton is a passionate soul. A man that the tabloid press has jabbed more swipes at than punches Floyd Mayweather has landed, it's fair to say he's been through more public battles than most. The difference being, this opponent is standing strong on his feet, embracing the lessons learnt and the experience gained. A maverick or disruptor? He doesn't "give a shit".

"It was definitely the Italia 90 World Cup. I had the sticker book; it was the first time I was really interested in the kit, really interested in the players and what boots the players had on." Barton's face lights up as he begins to recall his earliest memories of football. For so many, whether you remember it or not, Italia 90 is earmarked by the heroics and passion of Paul Gascoigne, something that Barton appreciates, but it's another free spirit that he chooses to highlight. "I think the whole thing about Cameroon in that tournament [stands out] – they beat Argentina early on and Roger Milla captivated everyone." Equally, typified by his appreciation for New Order / Keith Allen's 'World in Motion', as well as the iconic Umbro England kits of the time, he's a man of eclectic tastes.

Naturally you begin to wonder if he managed to complete the sticker album. "No – I never had enough money. I used to rob a bit of money out of my mum's purse and stuff when she wasn't looking to get stickers, but never ever near enough to complete the sticker book."

Four years down the line, and no place for England at USA 94 following a failed qualifying campaign. Despite England's absence, it was a tournament Barton found himself immersed in, and one player in particular captured his mind. "I loved Georghe Hagi and the way he wore his socks cut off. I remember asking that Christmas for the Lotto Stadia he used to wear – I was obsessed with him and that Romanian side."

"Football, style and music go hand in hand – think soccer casuals. If I hadn't been a football player then that's what I would have been."

—

Barton's career is one that has been peppered with controversy; like many, he has had his demons. On the pitch scuffles, off the pitch jail-time – the picture painted is one of a menace. However the truth is there to see. Proving to be a commanding player, captaining Premier League sides, he has defied many a doubter. There's far more between the ears than the cannon fodder-filled papers might lead you to believe.

Going back to his formative years, the limelight is something that has echoed on many occasions. "I remember Mrs Swift at Beckets (St Thomas Becket High School) – she wanted me to be in the school play, so I went [along] because there were a few decent girls in it. All of a sudden she wanted me to be lead role in Oliver Twist, and I was like, 'Miss I'm too cool, I'm not getting up and singing in front of the whole school and all that.'" A consumer of culture, his image is diverse. "At the time I was building a bit of a reputation [as] a tough tackling kind of local hard man on the football pitch, and I think being in the school play might have ruined my brand."

A brand that has been through the wash several times over, Barton is an example of modern football. Having been told at a young age that he wouldn't fit the mould or, more specifically, the height of a professional player, he broke convention, eventually rising through youth academy ranks. His climb to established Premier League Player is well documented: Everton and Liverpool at youth level, then onto Man City, Newcastle, QPR and now most

recently, Burnley. He's older, wiser and offering more commentary on the situation the game finds itself in than ever. What's more, he realises just how tough the journey is. "It's not an easy profession. So many young dreams and ambitions start out on a journey, wanting to be a footballer, and there are pitfalls all along the way. I think more so now than ever it's becoming more and more difficult."

Barton airs his concern about the way in which players are brought through in England. "My fear is, I think what we're setting these kids up to do, is not play football. We're teaching them to play football the wrong way. I think it's all good and well we're teaching them about possession and the importance of keeping the ball, but that only works for a small percentage of them, because only a small percentage of them are going to have the opportunity to play in the Premier League against other teams that do that and on surfaces that allow that to happen."

It's a convincing argument. With the game varying so much outside the top flight, it's what happens when players drop to lower leagues that's the main issue. "They run into what's happening in the real world, where for some parts of the game the ball might not even touch the ground, and they have no plan B. All of a sudden their confidence breaks down – they actually start to think, 'I'm not as good as I thought I was.'"

Clearly an area of great importance, as he explains. "I say this very mindfully, but I think what some

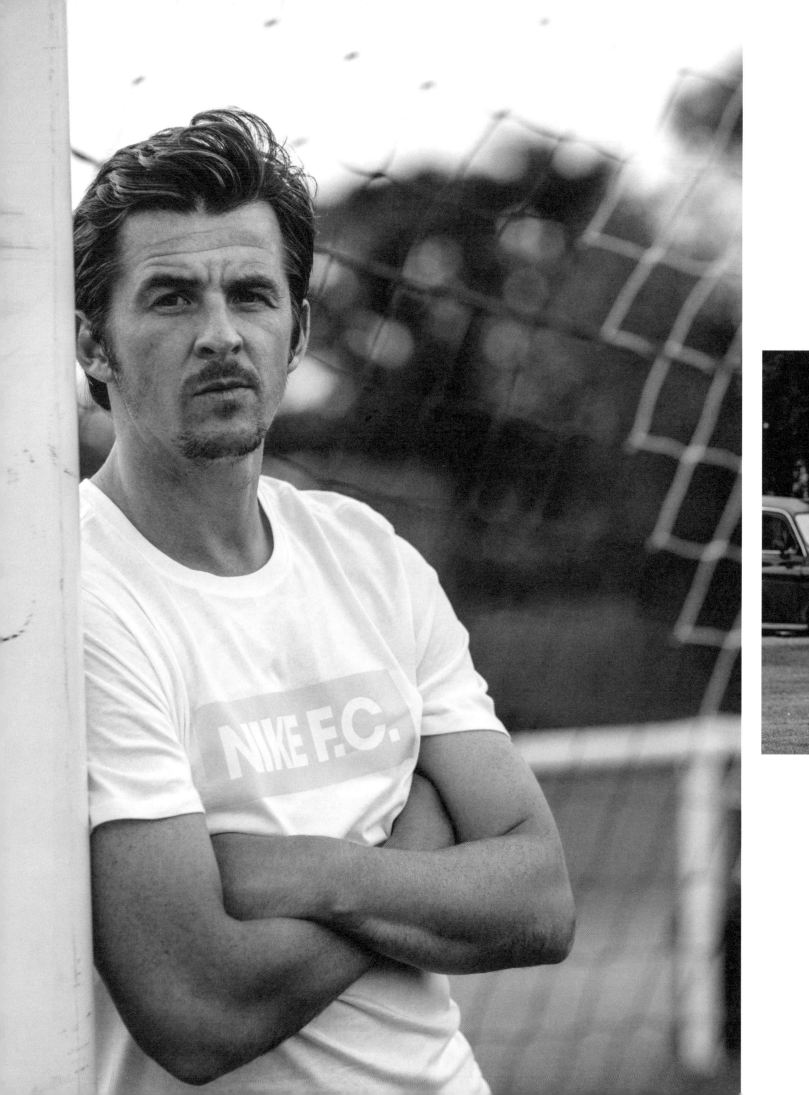

organisations are doing borderlines on neglect." A strong believer in the work that coaches do, it is the administrative side that he feels lets the side down. "You can't have great players without great coaches, and you can't have great coaches without great players. We haven't got that now: we've got forms you've got to fill in and checklists you've got to tick off. It's sad; and I really, really feel for these kids. It's not like they're any less talented or less driven than other generations."

"For someone who has played in the Premier League for the majority of their career, I think the standard is certainly dipping, or the strength in depth of the standard is certainly on the wane. I think [these are] worrying times for English football, which has been highlighted by the debacle that was the last World Cup."

Emphasising that all is not lost however, his faith remains in untamed players coming through and beating the system. "Players like Jamie Vardy and Charlie Austin. To see two kids drop to the lower echelons and grind their way back to the top – it shows that there are going to be countless players that slip through the cracks. It's a strange period for English football – we've almost got into the process of the industrial revolution for players."

"I think we could be in danger of making things too structured. Some of our best players are players that aren't conventional; Wayne Rooney [was] the stereotypical street footballer when he came through."

"I could rock up to most academies and have a pot shot at what your number six will look like, what your number eight will look like, what your centre-half will look like. Where's the USP for these players? We don't really know what to do with flair players. We never have."

Left A fan first and foremost his opinions stand strong. An inquisitive thinker.

Above Never one to turn down a kick-about. Joey downs tools and gets involved.

"The great managers over the years – Wenger, Ferguson – have understood the need for a maverick: someone who will go in there and win a game. A Cantona, a Thierry Henry, a Bergkamp – this kind of player that is the opposite [of] the norm. Someone who steps out against it. You look at the national team, and it's stale."

Not simply here to state opinion, his views do not come without offered solutions. He is someone who embraces the changes that he believes the game should buy into. "We need technology – it shouldn't be the luckiest team that wins." He acknowledges the steps that have already been taken – the vanishing spray used for freekicks is "a good invention" – but thinks that the major decisions in a game need greater attention. "Goals, penalties and red cards. I think yellow cards, offsides and so on should be left to the officials because on the whole they get a lot of stuff right. The media simply highlight the stuff they get wrong."

"The game is so fast now. The athletic profile of the players is going north and I feel sorry for the referees because they're not elite level athletes. They're getting fitter, they're professional – but not all of them. The surfaces we're playing on, the balls we're using, the kits we're in – everything is becoming lighter and [more] about the power to weight ratio. It's all about faster, faster, faster, so obviously it's going to be more difficult for the human eye – the referee's eye – to pick up every decision and get every decision correct."

"We need to think about using technology to help the referees and help them make the best calls. If the referee wants a little bit of help then it doesn't mean they are crap. Often that's what people think we're saying."

"We're saying we want them to make the right decision; we want the best team to win, not the luckiest team. You don't want the refs to be castigated and struck off the list and all these things that come with it. You've seen it; you know, the lynch mob come out when the ref has made a couple of bad decisions. Let's help them: help them make the best decisions. I think it's completely rational to do it."

"Some people are saying, 'Don't mess with football, it doesn't need altering' – we've got to move with the times. We've got to try and level the playing field."

"It's criminal that in this country where we have so many people that love football, we're pricing them out of it. I think it's a disgrace."

—

Naturally for players and fans alike, on the pitch matters are a priority. It is after all the game we pay to see. However, like the rest of us, at heart Joey Barton is a football fan. He cares about the bigger picture, off the pitch in the stands, just as much as the moments when you cross over the line. "Off the pitch we should really [focus on] having full stadiums. We shouldn't be pricing fans out of football. I think we should be very conscious [of] what's going on in the economy, and I think clubs should make a better effort to accommodate supporters because it's a two way street."

With TV revenues providing such a lucrative source of income for the game, it is hard to imagine why, in a world where football is such a valuable currency of passion, seats are ever empty in a stadium. TV revenues are where they are simply because it is a game that people want to watch. "There's nothing worse than playing in a half-empty stadium. Why should there ever be an empty seat in a stadium? The demand for seats is high so it could only be a cost point."

Joey Barton's focus is very much on the game. He champions many a change and you cannot fault his passion as it comes from a genuine place. The place of a fan. This fan is just a little more high profile than most. The profile is the price you pay in being a modern day football player, especially if controversy off the pitch ensues. In Joey's case, run-ins with the law meant he was a sitting duck waiting to be shot at. Nowadays, as a result of his twenties, pretty much anything he says can be taken, twisted and used as ammunition, and it's not something he mixes his words about.

"The media on the whole are governed by what they get fed – they're part of the game. They'll leak information and it'll be a two way street. That's the world we live in – whether they want to tell the truth or not. There [are] some great journalists out there who do tell the truth, but on the whole they are governed by whoever owns the paper and the agenda they set."

A strong opinion this maybe, however this is where the mature and composed Joey Barton takes the stage. He knows that without smoke in the early days, there would be no fire now. "At the end of the day, you are the master of your own destiny." Having grown up and found his feet, taming the fires in the process, his current mind frame is one of acceptance. "Someone like me, who was in an awful lot of trouble ... at some stage you need to draw the line and say, 'Okay, I've got to get my shit together here.'"

Open and honest, he explains how his world could have gone south before it even took flight. "I could name you five or six kids off our estate who were phenomenal players, a lot better football players than me, who in the end never played a league game because they couldn't behave themselves. It's easy to blame circumstances – it would be dead easy for me to blame my circumstances, dead easy. But you can't. You've got to look yourself in the mirror and say, 'You're the master of your own destiny.' " In print it may read like emotive cheese but there is genuine conviction here. Some wise words from an experienced head.

Football has been the lifeline for Joey Barton. "It got me off St. John's estate; it broadened my horizons." His pathway could have taken a completely different course and, having made mistakes along the way, winning or failing, his advice is free. "You have to say, 'What is it that I want to achieve?' You find that young kids are generally naïve: they make a lot of mistakes because that's what we do. I think it's your attitude to learning from mistakes."

Turning things around is not always plain sailing, and football is perhaps one of the most unforgiving places to craft a career. "I found that in the summer trying to get a club. People [thought] Hannibal Lecter was going to turn up; it's a lazy industry where people will believe what they read in papers." It is a short game with a long memory. With a Championship club to his name who are fighting for a return to the top flight, he has the opportunity to positively help write the headlines once more.

It is at this point, putting headlines aside, that we have the opportunity to get to go a little further into the mind of Joey Barton. A thinker, he describes himself as having an inquisitive personality. Music plays a big part in his cultural make-up. "The first single I bought was Billy Joel, 'We Didn't Start The Fire'. It seems bad now. I missed The Smiths first time around, completely missed them: I was far too

young when they came around." His musical voyage of discovery started, like many of us, with "The Charlatans, Oasis, Paul Weller." Famed for quoting many a Smiths lyric across social media, his musical net of reach is far more widespread. Much like his World Cup icons, it's the alternative nature that he appreciates. "The fact that they weren't really cool, that everyone thought that they were like suicide music – they really polarised opinion. It's really great music. There's no doubt about it, Marr and Morrissey together. Phenomenal." With his grandad introducing him to Bob Dylan, his parents big into Motown, and his uncle embedded into the rave scene the likes of The Stone Roses and Happy Mondays led, it gives a snapshot into a genre-crossing influence.

With the future yet to be defined for Barton, there's clearly a drive to offer his services back to the game. "Some footballers are very quick to say, 'I don't love football, it's a job for me' – it's bollocks. I love football. This is something I think I have to give back to, it's given me an awful lot in my life. I don't intend to take everything and run, and sit in a mock Tudor castle somewhere and reminisce about how good I was."

And while he jests. "I'll probably be painting fucking road markings, who knows. Life is very, very fragile." It comes with an astute understanding. Referencing the likes of Matthew Syed's book 'Black Box Thinking', which encourages learning from failure, it is a knowledgeable and pragmatic approach to the future.

The board laid out though unwritten, Joey Barton will continue to challenge opinion. On a mission to give something back, whether it's grass roots or in the professional game, it won't be his teeth carrying the venom. "Life is very much like a game of snakes and ladders; for me it's about staying on the ladders and avoiding the snakes. I've stepped on one or two fucking anacondas over the years. Now I've learnt my way of negotiating through, I'm climbing ladders at a rapid rate, so long may it continue."

"I don't intend to take everything and run and sit in a mock Tudor castle somewhere and reminisce about how good I was."

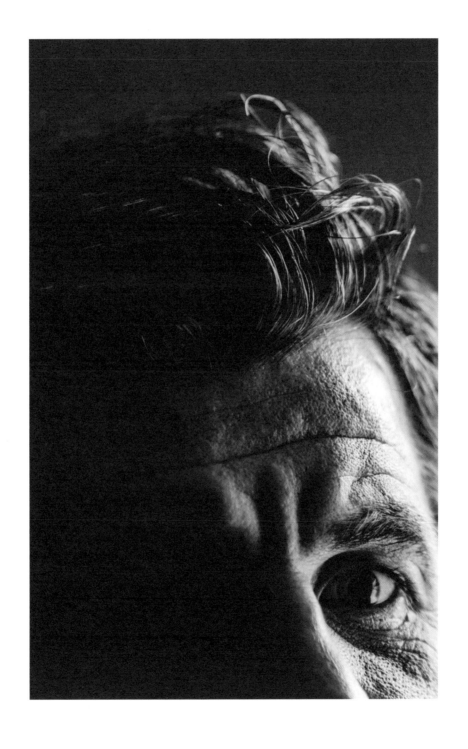

ALONE RANGER

—

Nile Ranger

Photography by Mehdi Lacoste

Disorder and disruption have shadowed Nile Ranger throughout his career, but now he's ready to right the wrongs and pull himself back up the metaphorical football cliff from which he hangs.

Outfit by True Religion

"I need this season, it's my biggest yet. I'm not getting any younger, so it's make or break."

—

It's now or never for Nile Ranger, the once highly-rated youngster leading the line at Newcastle United in the Premier League who scored at Stamford Bridge and represented England at youth level. While his ability has never been doubted, Ranger's career has been littered with off-pitch controversy and as a result, at the age of twenty four, his future as a professional hangs in the balance. Managers consider him a risk. And in football risks can be expensive.

In the past Ranger has been easy pickings for newspapers and some supporters have even written off his career. And if you believe everything you read in the papers then you might question whether he has what it takes to turn things around. But Ranger is now determined to fulfil his potential and he's in a reflective mood when he meets us in London for Monday morning tea and cake. Obviously.

"People don't see the other side of me. They only see what the media publish [and] the media always target me. I can drop a piece of cake on the floor and the media will blow it massively out of proportion. I'm used to that now, but it makes getting clubs difficult because I have got baggage and I understand that. I'm a lively character but I feel misunderstood."

As it stands Ranger is contracted to Blackpool, a club struggling on and off the pitch with a squad in desperate need of goals and difficulties of a financial nature. But Ranger is nowhere near the squad and, once again, it's not his ability that's the problem – it's a lack of trust influenced by his off-field antics.

"I've got one more year at Blackpool and after that I can leave. But right now it's not happening. I'm a no-one to the manager. I went up there and the manager said he didn't want me in his plans, even though I'm probably one of his best strikers. I do understand it because I went AWOL for a bit but there was so many other issues going on that were deeper than that. But I went back up there knowing I had to be the bigger man and do my job but it didn't work out. They sent me home [and] said get back in your car and drive back to London. I asked the club if they can release me from my contract but the chairman said no. I'm on hardly anything at Blackpool, it's pay-as-you-play, so it's peanuts. I think they're doing it to spite me but that's how it goes. I don't like the way Blackpool are treating me but I appreciate that I still have a contract there."

Ranger tripped almost accidentally into the football industry. As a talented youth player his path into football was already set in stone and, since it wasn't something he had to work particularly hard for, it could be attributed to his lack of focus in the past. But, as he says now, the penny has dropped and it's time to work hard, bring the right attention and be around the right people.

"I have grown up but I've got to focus [and] I've had to cut out a lot of people from my life. For example, I don't go on nights out anymore and it'll be worth it at the end of the day because I can chill in London and do what I want after my career. Football is such a short career but all it takes for me is to get a chance because I know my abilities. I just need to show everyone that I've changed and I'm ready to fully focus on football."

To us, Nile doesn't come across as a man who has a problem with authority. Having read a lot of stories on his character, we'd perhaps naively assumed we'd be meeting a player with arrogance but that wasn't the case. As he admits he has a history and not a pretty one, but the guy pouring tea on the other side of the table and offering us a slice of cake was polite, chilled-out and open to talk about anything.

When we questioned Nile about his fragmented career, he invariably exhibited a sense of bemusement and seemingly couldn't grasp why there had been so many obstacles in his way. Eventually, though, an answer would prevail and a realisation of his mistakes would emerge. "I can't put my finger on it. Every time something good is going to happen to me it's shut down. There's so many opportunities that I could go through like [when I was] about to sign for Leeds and a few other clubs, but it always gets stopped just as I'm about to go through the door. I don't know why. Everyone is scared to take the risk because I got in bother when I was young and when the money was coming in. My friends were like 'let's party, let's do everything' and it was all happening so I just said let's do it, let's live. I thought it would be like that forever but that's not the case."

It's well-known that young players who sign a cash-covered contract and start taking home the big money can very often become vulnerable to temptation and some deal with their newfound fame and fortune better than others. For Ranger, however, he was living the dream and thinking short term, ignoring advice given to him by team-mates and managers. "I remember Kevin Nolan saying to me, 'If you carry on the way you are, you're going to be doing nothing in two years.' I'd laugh and dismiss it, but he was right."

"Footballers are different. When I meet with my friends who I grew up with I have to realise that I'm different to them. I'm watched by the public, so if they're doing something mischievous they can get away with it and it's quickly forgotten about, but if I do it it's all over the paper. I now realise that."

The last couple of seasons have been a wake-up call for Ranger as he's slipped down the leagues and seen his wage lose a zero each step down. Could he still force his way into Blackpool's plans? Who knows? We're only hearing his side of the story. There could be an underlying stubbornness from the player or it could be simple and that Blackpool have made their decision clear. So who offers Ranger support

at this time? "My family have pushed me, my mum especially. She's always saying, 'Go back up to Blackpool, even if you have to train by yourself, just go back up!' People will ask me on the street what's going on with football, but it's out of my hands. Obviously that gets annoying, but I have to deal with it properly and explain the situation and thank them for caring and that it means a lot."

If a club did offer Nile an opportunity it would be headlined as a lifeline, but there's still an ambition inside him that aims high. "I just want to get back into it. I'd like a decent Championship club. I just need a team and a good manager to trust me. I've spoken to a few managers and I've told them that the penny has dropped now, that I was living recklessly but now I'm ready to settle down and focus."
"In five years' time I want to be back in the Premier League. That's my aim but it's going to be hard. I'm still confident in my ability [and] any doubts

"I've had more lives than a cat. I've had so many chances and I think I've got one more"

managers have had in my career have been due to my off-field behaviour. They'd tell me all the time but it used to go in one ear and out the other. Managers would tell me to sort myself out and I'd be like, 'yeah, yeah, yeah,' and then get in trouble for going out when I wasn't supposed to. At Newcastle they'd have a guy who would go around the nightclubs and wait there to see if players turned up. Alan Shearer did that when we got relegated and players would get huge fines. I got dropped and had to train with the academy for two weeks."

The purity of football that Ranger saw and enjoyed as a kid has become increasingly murky as a consequence of his own decisions and the political world of the sport on the wrong side of the white line. For a player with such a point to prove, he'll only be able to resurrect his career if he genuinely wants it, plays for the right reasons and still has a love for the game. "I did lose my love for it but I know I love it again because I miss it so much. I want to be back out there doing what I'm supposed to be doing. But football isn't black and white, it's not that easy. There's lots of other things going on. God willing something will come along."

Piece of cake: Nile Ranger
meets us for Monday
morning tea at MADD
Hatter's Café, London.

There's a mixture of denial and blame and sometimes a sense of pride around the predicaments of his youth, but he speaks about those events in a past tense now as if it's all behind him and he's working on a clean page. "I brought it on myself with all the trouble I used to get into but I'm not the complete bad boy the media made me out to be anymore. I grew up with people who were getting in trouble and it's taken me time to realise that but I've separated from them now. I'm on a different path to them now [and] I've got a better understanding of what is expected from a professional."

Ranger can talk all he wants about his determination to get back on the rails he fell off so many times, but he needs to return to the pitch, behave and let his football do the talking. He's made his career complicated and it's understandable that clubs are cautious and see him as a gamble. As he says, he comes with baggage – avoidable baggage that he shouldn't have picked up. But with experience comes knowledge, which can be passed on and used in a positive way if he shows regret and ultimately grows from it. So what advice would Nile give to an 18-year-old version of himself?

"I'd tell him to focus on the ball. There are so many distractions – girls, clubbing, money, gambling – you need to be careful and just love the game and it'll come. Don't think about wanting money or anything like that, think about the ball and all that other stuff will come secondary. Always keep football the primary motivation."

"I've had more lives than a cat. I've had so many chances and I think I've got one more and when it comes I'm going to grab it with both hands. I'll take it." If he does, fair play; if he doesn't, he'll know who to blame. It's time to take responsibility. If he's right and he does in fact have one more round at last-chance saloon, what sort of player would a club be getting? One with a point to prove, according to Ranger. "I'd be hungry man. I realise now that this career is short and you need to give it everything. In twenty years' time I want to be remembered as the guy who turned it around, the man who did it, he started well then went downhill but he finished at the top." If his career was a film then that would be the perfect script, but this is real life and it's going to be a steep climb. It's time to watch that dwindling flame either intensify into a roaring fire or fizzle out.

HARD KNOX

—

Storelli

Storelli are the new boys making big noise in New York by tackling the lonely world of football injuries with a protection collection built to withstand the physicality of the game. Lightweight and innovative, Storelli keep your foot firmly on the accelerator while offering a seat belt that keeps you on the road for even more miles.

The brand are investing a whole lot of research, development and money in creating products with the sole aim of maximising your season through injury prevention. Action not reaction.

Like Under Armour and Nike, Storelli was founded by former athletes on a mission to revolutionise the performance equipment market. With an emphasis on performance, as well as a higher purpose that involves being the best you can be, Storelli are forging their

own path with radical design and creative solutions built on a disruptive mentality, as Chief Marketing Officer Mark Schermers tells us.

"Our founders, Claudio Storelli and Jing Liang, played together at New York's Chelsea Piers. They and their team-mates would often pick up injuries and felt that the psychological effects of getting injured were just as great as the physical. Whilst the game and players have evolved in recent years, the equipment wasn't keeping up. Players at every level are shelling out hundreds of dollars for boots, but there wasn't a brand serving products with a protective component to keep them on the pitch and in those boots."

Like many underdog brands, Storelli has an attitude. Straight out of Brooklyn, New York, the hardscrabble city has helped shape the brand's identity. "We have certainly embraced Brooklyn as a part of our company DNA. Football has never been a hotter

topic in New York than it is now and the timeliness of our arrival drives us to think differently about how to launch our football brand. With New York as our backdrop, we are focused on promoting our products in the context of the 'Gotham Side of Football', inviting players around the world to see the beautiful game from our unique perspective."

A lot of companies talk about innovation and disruption, but few take the risk to really make bold leaps. Storelli are making moves with the aim of changing the game in the athletic gear business. "Brands have boot tunnel vision. That's where we keep seeing innovation, and we can hardly blame them – that's where the money is. Making mainstream protection, or rather, making protection mainstream, is a more expensive proposition."

New technology has traditionally been slow to be embraced in football, and Storelli are under no illusions that their path into the game will be

easy. The brand essence revolves around being the underdog, being hungry and competing against the best. "Success won't happen overnight," admits CEO Claudio Storelli. "We've found a very receptive ear in the MLS who have been at the forefront of innovation in the game, and we find that there is a new breed of coaches who are all too aware of the costs of having their players watching injured from the sidelines. We loathe to be a fearmongering company, but we do feel a responsibility to players to lay out the facts and to keep innovating our gear based on the feedback we get from them."

Storelli are hardly the first brand with ambitions to disrupt an industry, but with a brand portfolio that provides energy and differentiation from imitators, the opportunity is there. "There is a sea of sameness out there and the category is ripe for disruption," Claudio explains. "When a market is dominated by a select few brands focused on limited product categories, innovation suffers and there is a demand for something unexpected. We believe only a challenger brand has the opportunity to serve the untapped needs of the everyday athlete. We know we will become a big player in the football world not by shelling out hefty endorsements, but by gaining credibility, leading innovation and offering every player a distributive voice."

The US company exemplify authenticity and personality without being budget-busting. They've gone from a small start-up to one of the industry's most exciting new brands. It might seem natural to assume that a brand with a focus on protection would be associated with American football or rugby,

"Our gear has to feel like a second skin. It can't hinder — it's more protection in disguise."

but that's a dated mindset — the emphasis is fully on football. "Storelli is made by and for football players, it's that simple. Our gear is designed in Brooklyn and tested daily on pitches nearby. We get immediate feedback on our gear and make changes accordingly. We don't believe in gimmicks. Every panel on our gear is designed to solve a specific need — whether that be nasty tackles to the lower legs, turf burn injuries from sliding or heavy impact blows to the torso or head."

Storelli continues to look beyond itself in order to serve a higher purpose, and for a newcomer, brand feedback is the most important ingredient for progression. "Players are attracted to the bold, stealth design of the products, but it's the fit, comfort and technical components of our designs that stick. This has a lot to do with sourcing ultra lightweight materials and fitting them to the contours of a football player's body. Footballers are shocked by the lightness, considering every product has a protective layer to withstand high levels of impact.

Visually, the Storelli collection packs a stealth-like vibe, and that's very much down to the design philosophy of the brand, underpinned by the premise that players don't want to feel like they're wearing protection. "Our gear has to feel like a second skin. It can't hinder and is more protection in disguise. As a result, from a design point of view, most of our gear is very stealth looking, almost hidden away, which is the case for most of our BodyShield products. Our brand has a bright future and we have plans for making protection more visible with 'louder' designs. We'll have some fun with it, but won't lose our form or function."

Above BodyShield Knee Guard
Left BodyShield GK 3/4 Undershirt
Top Right BodyShield Leg Sleeve & BodyShield Sliders
Bottom Right ExoShield GK Gladiator Jersey

Storelli have put in all the groundwork before launch. Unlike numerous wannabe breakthrough brands, Storelli have found their identity – they know who they are and what they want to achieve. They're prepared. Everything is in place for them to have a real crack at the football industry and to stand tall while others have face-planted over the first hurdle.

So what's next? The brand have set a high bar for the future. "We hope to see the brand present on all football pitches across the world in the next ten years. We will likely be seen more as a sports technology brand than a protection brand by then, adapting to the needs of the 'Next-Gen' athlete. Most of all, we hope to keep our edge and stick to our roots as a challenger brand that is still fundamentally striving to make next-generation products to allow the best players in the world to keep playing at their best."

Play on.

DEFYING CONVENTION

—

PUMA Headquarters

A fight for the avante-garde, challenging the rules is not necessarily something taught. With a passion for defying convention we headed to PUMA HQ getting our take on a brand that has influenced a change on the game on countless occasions.

RUDOLF DASSLER HALL

"Our strategy is about being progressive, not just accepting the status quo..."

—

Terence Parris

Our host at this lab of creativity is one Terence Parris. Head of Marketing Teamsport he is a man of great experience. Joining the brand in 2001 he was right in the mix up until 2006 at which point he was head-hunted by Apple. Taking the opportunity to contribute to a different industry, learning all the while, he moved back to PUMA after two years with the tech power house. Inspiration drawn from a brand of such might and combining this for the world of football can only lead to interesting places.

A lean office, Terence is proud of his "core team of six, we are small but we shout loud". There's no denying that. Many a dent has been marked on the more suited side of football with the help of PUMA. It is a game after all - albeit one of monumental athleticism and PUMA is a brand that continues to pack a disruptive punch on a heavyweight pitch.

PUMA is a brand that stands out as a truly unique innovator. How would you define the PUMA football strategy?
We've recently re-set our football strategy to be the most progressive football brand in the world. At one time, our aim was to be the clear number three. We are the clear number three although you shouldn't be complacent as there are some new brands in the

market and some existing brands that have been really performing well. But when you look at our history, whether it has been conscious or not, we have created quite a distinct position as a football brand, so calling ourselves 'the most progressive football brand' does really personify who we are as a brand.

We've always been synonymous with innovation, not necessarily going against the rules but kind of challenging convention. So our strategy is certainly about being progressive, not just accepting the status quo. Certainly in the early years of PUMA, when you look at our competitors, we definitely had an ability to identify with the most iconic footballers of a generation and so, for example, if you look right up to 'modern football', the top five or six most iconic players, probably in the whole of football history, we have all but one of those.

So as I say, whether that was a strategic decision or not, we definitely were the brand that identified with the game changer. I kind of tease the guys here because I have been wearing PUMA since 1973 and, for me personally, PUMA has always been a brand that has identified itself with individually minded, game changer type of players.

Going against the grain seems to be a recurring theme running through the vast array of products that have been released by PUMA. From a design perspective, where do you think the brand gets that rebellious edge from?

It's one of the most difficult things to answer, because I don't think we have set our stall out to specifically be the most unconventional or to go against the rules. One of the things I ask people we interview is how they see PUMA against other brands. One of the personal perspectives I have is that, when you look at other brands, we're the only animate brand - we're the only one that is effectively an animal with a soul - and I do feel that there is a specific soul to PUMA that other brands don't have. Often, people that survive and do well at PUMA tend to feel that soul, rather than just kind of collect a pay cheque because you can go other places where you can get a better pay cheque.

My very personal perspective is that there is a soul of PUMA that people either get or don't get and over the years it has driven design inspiration, driven the type of athletes that we have endorsed, the

federations that we have been associated with - you take Jamaica as an example - I would say that Jamaica is one of the coolest countries in the world and performs disproportionately bigger than its size and Italy is one of the most iconic cultured countries in the world.

PUMA Football has well and truly carved its name into the history books. Is leaving a legacy a must when looking to design new products?

It's kind of funny. I had a conversation with a talented friend of mine once who said he 'wanted to be great' and I reflected on that statement and you look at history. History is full of great people who believed in doing what they loved best. It was history that defined them as great. So I don't think people design with a view to legacy, they design with a view to passion and beauty that is reflective of a legacy so I would say that we have people here who are passionate about what they do, do it to the very best of their ability, have that PUMA soul that I referred to, and that combination creates great things that become a legacy.

PUMA HQ. Making their mark, one dynamic move after the next. Oh that? Just Pele.

From the likes of Cruyff and Maradona right through to Agüero - When it comes to collaborating with players, are they cherry-picked to ensure they share that soul?

More so now. There was a period where we probably couldn't afford to compete with some of our competitors. But again we are lucky in that some footballers see and understand PUMA and want to be associated with a brand that fits their personality. So it fluctuates between us identifying people who suit and those who see us as a brand that they want to be associated with, and not just by how much we can afford to pay them, so it's definitely a combination of both.

We've always had a history of great players, but at this particular moment our collective portfolio is the best it has ever been, full of people that not just tick the box - you look at Sergio Agüero and the way he plays, with his tongue sticking out like a kid - that is who we are. As a brand, we've got competitors across the road who are a machine and another who is all about being the number one. We do it with a smile on our faces and Sergio Agüero personifies that.

From those famous Rigobert Song Tricks Kings, the sleeveless Cameroon kits through to the Balotelli Mohawk boots most recently, is it part of the brand's ethos and mentality to keep dropping in these statement pieces?

Yes, definitely, though one of the things that sometimes gets lost in those stories is the performance component. So, for example, when you look at both the Cameroon sleeveless shirts and Uni

QTs, they are both performance-based enhanced products. Take the uni-kit as an example; it was an all-in-one kit that had the cycling short element. That was at a period where a lot of players were wearing that sort of under garment so we simply integrated that into a kit. It wasn't a gimmick. It was definitely a performance-inspired design so we will continue that.

You look at the current Arsenal kits and, in fact now all of our teams, people comment on the tight fitted-ness through our ACTV technology. Yes, it shows off their physique but there is actually a performance component of combining compression with taping that a lot of players use around their bodies to stimulate the muscles and improve the performance. So yes, there are things like the Balotelli Mohawk boots that, to an extent, are gimmicky but our designs, as quirky as they may seem, have had a performance foundation to them. We may need to be careful that isn't lost in that kind of "oh wow, PUMA's doing something wacky" because 80% of ideas are rooted in genuine performance enhancement aspirations.

Looking at all those examples that PUMA has brought the world - screw in studs is a prime example. What would you say is the biggest game changer that PUMA brought to the world of football?

There are almost too many to mention. For me, probably because of my childhood, I would say PUMA's legacy is King. That's very much a personal perspective though. I hope we will continue to find a way to keep King fresh and relevant and appealing. It continues to have the ability to be a game changer for the kid that doesn't want to wear a synthetic boot. Not that long ago, Alex Ferguson was complaining about the risk to young players that comes with boots from this day and age. I think King ticks the box in safety but not just that, it is genuinely a great boot. I think we have done a lot of great things over the years but if you were to ask me my favourite thing, it's the King.

In your entire PUMA career, is there one project you have worked on that you're most proud of?

I would say the current Arsenal project. It's ongoing. Not just the kit but all elements. It's been quite ironic but we've done big launches around the Arsenal kit that have have faced an industry criticism when other brands were so subtle in the way they launched kits of their big assets. I would say from a personal perspective that the criticism is actually based on an inability to better what we have done. Sometimes people only show humility because they have kind of run out of ideas. We needed to do something big to reset the dial in consumers' minds after so many years of a previous sponsor. I think to be critical of what we did reflects the success of what we achieved.

So I think that the way we have launched Arsenal, everything from the imagery that we have created, the launch film, the launch event, the assets, the stories. I mean, season one, we had the April Fools' Stunt, the Arsene Wenger coat, the Ian Poulter golf viral and

that has been an opportunity for us to show just how good we can be across all areas - from design through to creative thinking to the way that we engage on social media platforms. So that's definitely one of my favourite things historically and we've still got many more years to follow.

What kind of person do you need to be to work at a brand like PUMA?

I think the people that do well as it were, really believe that they can make a change. They really feel PUMA and the soul of the brand. They are the people that recognise that the challenges we face are part of your job as opposed to obstacles that prevent you from doing your job. I think fundamentally they are people that are really passionate and it is a soul

that is hard to define but you've either kind of got it or not.

With Euro 2016 just around the corner, what can we expect from PUMA?

It's definitely going to be a busy couple of years. We potentially have five teams at the Euros which, again, when you look at the number of teams that will participate in the Euros, if we do have five, then as a percentage of participants it would be disproportionately bigger than we are in the market place. We have the reigning champions of AFCON and the three superpowers of African football. The 2017 AFCON is also the 20th anniversary of when we signed our first African team. So we definitely intend that to be big.

"You must be bold to dare wear a red boot on one foot and a yellow boot on the other foot. That was my personality, I was brave.

—

Rigobert Song

One man all too familiar with PUMA's non-conformist approach to football design is former Cameroon captain Rigobert Song. Almost two decades on from fearlessly stepping out at France '98 wearing odd boots, it's clear that, that single moment influenced the brand's attitude and rewrote the rules of football footwear design. Subsequently, PUMA's long-term relationship with a number of African nations has somewhat moulded its creative direction, perfectly capturing the colourful, extravagant and often experimental characteristics of African football in the process.

As an influential member of the Cameroon team during an extensive period between 1993 and 2010 that included 137 caps, Rigobert Song witnessed some of the most distinctively historic moments in the Cameroon/PUMA partnership. It included the now infamous vest jersey design, an array of insanely wild football boots and what has arguably become the most radical kit in the history of the game – so radical in fact that it was over-ruled by FIFA. The outrageously unconventional one-piece, merged shorts and shirt ensemble created a football kit/leotard combo that scared the living Djemba-Djemba's out of the old boys stuck in their ways at FIFA HQ. What became obvious with the speed at which they banned the kit is that they were never going to appreciate or understand the sort of boundary-pushing creativity for which PUMA had become known.

You originally wore these boots in the 1998 World Cup. What made you decide to wear one red boot and one yellow boot?

It was mainly because I felt really comfortable and at ease in those boots and I used to wear the King when I played for FC Metz in a very successful era right before the World Cup in France. I thought to myself, I have to wear a pair of boots that I am used to playing with and those colours were a perfect match for the Cameroon kit. Odd boots? Why not? There were no rules that said I couldn't. Football is fun and it's good to be creative.

Did the colour of the boots reflect your personality?

Yes it did. I believe one must have a strong personality because you must be bold to dare wear a red boot on one foot and a yellow boot on the other foot. That was my personality, I was brave. This bravery sprang from my life and it didn't bother me at all to wear those boots because I was already used to wearing PUMA. During my time at the FC Metz I'd sometimes wear red boots and sometimes wear yellow boots to match the Metz kits. Then I thought why not play with one red foot and one yellow foot? I think I was courageous to do that but courage is a part of football.

How did you feel when you found out PUMA was going to release the boots for the 2014 World Cup?

When I wore these boots back in 1998 I never thought that they would represent what they represent today. It totally came out of the blue, but I have a sense of pride about it and it's a great pleasure for me. I think PUMA always have the right reflex and that's what brings success to the brand, not only in Africa but in the whole world. PUMA is the brand that always had great inspiration and that little extra thing that you cannot explain but makes it different from other brands. It's truly unique.

What did you think of the 2002 Cameroon vest design when you first saw it?

PUMA have always been very creative with innovative models. I believe PUMA has always taken the extra step to do something special for us, for our image in Cameroon. They've always known how to work with us, how to answer our needs. In Africa it's very hot so the vest made sense and looked the part. I loved it and it was nice that PUMA were thinking about our comfort and all the players felt great wearing it.

For the 2002 World Cup were you disappointed when FIFA said that you couldn't wear the sleeveless design?

We were very comfortable with those jerseys. We won the 2000 Africa Cup of Nations wearing it, but FIFA decided we could not play with a sleeveless jersey and PUMA came up with an option to put some black sleeves on them, which we were happy to play in for that World Cup in South Korea/Japan. But it was a shame we couldn't wear the original design.

You're Cameroon's most capped player. How does that make you feel?

Brazil is talked about a lot in terms of football as the football nation, but in Africa Cameroon in particular is a football nation where people love the game, so I'm incredibly proud to be the most capped player and to have experienced so much in my time with the national team. Cameroon has taken part in seven World Cups and that's huge for Africa, and it also means that we are consistent. Now we have to go beyond simply participating and try to go as far as possible.

Borussia Dortmund

Photography by James Hendley
Type by Crush Creative

We went to Signal Iduna Park to get our taste, and it's true what they say. Like being thrust face-to-face with a well-nourished, albeit caged, lion – content, beautiful and dressed so rich in colour – its presence is ready to roar once more. Sheer ecstasy instantly captures the senses. On the menu for this carnivorous king of cultured football is the Bundesliga. A feast of affordable, well supported and nurtured passion, it's the perfect celebration of the unique qualities this game possesses. We went behind the scenes at BVB to paint the genuine picture, to showcase why this is simply not a hipster club for the masses, but a mecca for the football appreciator.

Dortmund is a club well-written and, equally, the Bundesliga and its accessibility is something that the world of football often turns to as a point of inspiration. The envy of many clubs with fans all over the globe, it is one that runs as an efficient business of self-sufficiency. Enduring a turbulent past, it has not been plain sailing for the Borussia Dortmund, fighting back from the brink of extinction as financial woes spiraled. It is over the last 10 years that fortunes have favoured the brave, and brave they have been.

Title wins, cup trophies, financial stability and the departure of one Jurgen Klopp, the past 5 years perhaps embody the dynamism that befits BVB.

Offering a dosage of visionary thinking from behind the scenes, BVB's Director of Sales & Marketing, Carsten Cramer gives a fascinating insight as to what helps a club of such maverick tendencies tick. "I got the offer from the CEO to join the club as responsible for all the marketing and brand activities in October 2010. It was the right moment to jump on the train".

Football is very much an all-or-nothing world and to succeed demands commitment, which is something Carsten shares. "If you work for a club like this you have to be fully passionate about it [and] it's always more than 9-5. Honestly it's 24/7. This club is never treated like a daily business – it's a lifestyle, it's something you take home with you, at all times." On a fundamental level, the day-to-day role of Cramer is to develop and gain suitable and sustainable business for now and for the future as he explains, "it is very important for the club. It's not just about money; we also want to develop the value of the brand so we have to know what our club stands for. We want to find the right partners who understand what we stand for. Whatever we do has to be sustainable. We're not interested in short term development. We want to reach credibility. The main characteristics of BVB are the authenticity, the intensity of the experience of being at a game. To be ambitious, our club reaches many people, not only in Germany but also now in the UK and other places. Whatever we do we see how it would affect them. [For example] we don't like to increase ticket prices too much because you will build a distance between people and the club. We have to be a club for the people and we have to reach them emotionally."

A refreshing take on football. The business side, often blamed for detracting from the heritage of the game, making profit while providing the ultimate experience on and off the pitch is a remarkable feat. For BVB, it is about looking at themselves, not looking at other teams; they're purely interested in what is right for the club and the fans. "You have to know where you stand – don't race other people, just be confident in knowing where you stand. If you have your own mission and vision you can define your success by yourself. For us it was important to identify the DNA of BVB."

Said in a free thinking, unassuming fashion, there's no ignorance here. As Cramer explains, "Observation is always important. We never say that we know the right way and we know exactly how to do it. Mistakes can happen. We are very open-minded [and] the people are the club so you have to be open."

Perhaps the most iconic element of the BVB way of life is the shirt. Symbolic for the bold, bright yellow, they are everywhere in and around the stadium, a definitive form of expression. Pride like no other is worn when this shirt is pulled on and it is another element championed from the top. "Something that the new manager always said – the colour code is massive. The colours are not only unique, but very specific, maybe some of the secret of the emotional relevance of this club."

Going granular is something many fellow football aficionados will cherish. The sentiment at BVB is about dialling up a relationship, not simply one-sided marketing jargon or campaigning, and there is integrity at every turn. "It's part of BVB. We care on details, it's not just a shirt we want to sell to people, it's a piece of life. If

"We love to give people the feeling that match day is the best day of the week."
—

you have been in a financial situation like we have been, if you've been close to death you know what health means to you. We know that BVB is more than football for the fans." And although money may well be a global currency, football is the world's language. "We don't want to charge one supporter more money. We want more supporters in total." Once more, the perspective is a soothing refresher. "Football is the most valuable content wherever you go in the world. Football can be a substitution for music or religion to some people."

"We listen to fans and read their thoughts. We love to give people the feeling that match day is the best day of the week. We try to celebrate this day, the whole week boils up to kick off, the city becomes more yellow throughout the day and we care about that. The nearer we get to match day it becomes more and more about the football. When we hear good feedback from experiencing a game, it's confirmation for us that the way we celebrate football seems to be the right way."

A remarkable number, the club sits proud with 55,000 season ticket holders. The lifeblood of any club, it is these fans that are responsible for where the club is. They provide the foundation while people like Carsten steer the ship. It is not done alone, though.

Among the boots, shirts and nutritional must-haves, Kit Manager Frank Gräfen adds the final touches to the sanctuary of preparation that is the changing room. A place of worship, the spirit of the club bleeds in from the pitch, passing through the lenses of waiting

"We put in a great deal of effort and still rely on high tempo and emotion. You can't sit back and wait in front of 80,000 fans"

—

a sight of nonpareil. Not short of experience, Frank has held his role since 2004 and looks back fondly on many great moments shared. "The biggest moment was 2012 when we won the double, the championship and the cup and 2011, too, when we won the German Championship. We were doing open top bus tours around the city, so they were great days; big emotions that make the family big at BVB. The supporters we have every home game is around 81,000, which is incredible, but on the bus tours there was like 500,000 all over the streets of Dortmund. It was unique [and] the whole city was yellow and black."

A man of great stature and respect, Frank typifies the mentality of the club. Once working in the mining industry, backstage in the world of football is a juxtaposed change to comprehend. "I'm really proud to be part of the club and I've enjoyed every moment I've been here. I've got good relationships with everyone at the training facility, the players and the coaches, as well as the management who are always really respectable to each other, which makes life enjoyable. It's a 24/7 job, you need to be there when needed." Respect is the fundamental element that Frank is proud of, but it also takes a strong slice of trust to be let inside one of the world's most famous dressing rooms. With many big earners as well as egos coming through the door, it's

important for Frank to build a rapport with players early on. "I'm very open-minded with everyone. It's pretty simple; if somebody needs something then I am there to help on a regular and professional level. If you've got a job like mine, you can't admire too much, you can't look at the cars the players drive. They are earning a lot of money and you should be respectable of that otherwise you will admire too much."

The side of the game that Frank sees is acute and truly captivating. It is a role that is in much demand, and with players using anything from 30 to 70 shirts a season, the operation is of mammoth proportions. That's even before you consider the logistical requirements of transporting one of the world's biggest names around Europe. Keen to point out though, Dortmund is a club of collective might. "It's not only the big guys in front the camera. It's also the ones who do exhausting work which are extremely important for the club itself. Those guys behind the scenes sometimes start at 6am and they deserve huge respect. The groundsmen work in rain and cold and do their job perfectly just to prepare the pitch for the matches." It is this that speaks volumes. Those working at the club share the unrivalled passion for BVB as much as any fan.

A monumental
welcome. Signal Iduna
Park in all its glory.

If you took Borussia Dortmund and dropped them in the Premier League, they would look like a well-dressed game-changer. Not so much a rule breaker, more an adventurer or a pioneer. A close relationship with the fans means the engine is being powered by everyone who touches it. Everything is about a two-way dialogue. Several parts of Signal Iduna Park are 'Safe Standing' areas. Effectively fold away seats, it's a project that has been well-tested across the Bundesliga. Accompanying that, though, are traditional terraces. 'The Wall' looks no different to terracing that is known the world over – crash barriers chequer the enormous stand. However, it sits as part of a modern mega structure of a stadium and is managed carefully. Again, dialogue between fans and club is key.

Dortmund has been a club of impressive support for a considerable amount of time and the growth in fans it has experienced has broken many an expectation. Jens Volke describes his role as Supporter Liaison Officer to "stand as a link between the fans and the club. Our job is to network, to speak with both parts and communicate with the fans and with the club, bringing them together." A club that is so emphatically powered by the passions of its doting supporters, Jens' relationship with the club began over 30 years ago. Having bought his first season ticket in 1989, he was one of a record-breaking number. "At the time the German record was 11,000 season tickets - a record held by Borussia Dortmund and now we have 55,000."

Proud of the supporters he represents, Jens explains, "In Germany, there is no stadium that competes. Our supporters are very true. Even if we don't play good football, they are here, they are supporting the team. In the last 20 years we have only had a few matches when the fans have got angry and booed the team. We have those problems like most teams of course; if you have a passionate crowd it's always like you're dancing on a razor. It could be positive or it could be negative, but this happened only a few times over the last 30 years." This relationship between club and fans is special; working together for the greater good, there is a mutual understanding and respect for those employed by the club who are working behind the scenes and those on the terraces that make the club.

Not short of voice, much of the atmosphere and singing is driven by two guys that act as conductors to the crowd. Through megaphones and a PA system, which the club helped to construct, chants boom around the ground and bounce between various sets of fans. Sacrificing their view of the game, the leaders of voice are known as 'Capos'. "In the late 90s and into the new century we had a really weak atmosphere in the stadium. It was often so quiet and fans were only singing some popular pop songs. It was really quiet. So some fans and fan clubs founded together to build up a new group of supporters, and in the space of a year it changed into an ultra group. It was the biggest ultra group and called 'The Unity'. Both the guys

with the microphones were part of that [and] we talked to the club about building up a rig for the microphone and megaphone and the club trusted us. Since then, most of the fans know both the guys with the microphones. I think on one hand it's very important to have them because the atmosphere is very special and it's always loud for 90 minutes."

While Dortmund have seen many a World Cup winner pass through their doors, much of their nucleus is personified by one Marco Reus. As versatile as the club is at embracing its fans, Reus is a player with the pace and

"We try to be as authentic as possible, no artificial ideas."

agility to strike through many a defence. A maverick with his own style of play, his determination is compelling, "The best players in the world are hungry for success in every match and are all absolute team players. I firmly believe that you are nothing in football if you only think about yourself." Sharing the philosophy of the club, the winning mentality that focuses on the wider group, you can see why club and player are so well united."

Below Players show their appreciation the the fans
and soak up the support. So much mutual respect.

Speaking to him, his words resonated as a fan just as much as a player. "BVB is a big club, yet still a family. This family has provided the biggest average attendance in Germany for the last 17 years and for many years the biggest in Europe, too. This city is my home, the whole region lives for the club with every fibre in their body. But even though expectations have soared, the ten million or so Dortmund fans in Germany still managed to create a calm atmosphere of total support when we were suddenly bottom of the league last season. You only find that extreme bond here."

A success both on and off the pitch, much is owed to the open and honest relationships that have been shaped collectively. A match day 'experience' is simply too loose a word. Imagine you're at a gig and a cloud of heat sits nestled above, an unseen swell of atmosphere. Bustled together in constant anticipation, it is an adrenaline ride that will stay with you as you grow long in the tooth, and that is before we've even discussed a ball zipping across this beautifully maintained surface. Perhaps a sharp reminder that brings a welcome dose of perspective, as the final whistle to this journey draws near and beer flies over the shoulder in celebration of the 3rd BVB goal, we witness the fainting of a fan just yards ahead of where we stood. Immediately, like a family all looking out for one another, there is a rush of water brought forward to help the dehydrated supporter come back around. A touching moment amidst the passionate support that reminds you of the power of football, it will always be the fans that support the foundations and make this game so unique. Left to go home preaching the gospel of the game that is Borussia Dortmund, you are guaranteed to come back one item of yellow richer. From cake moulds to beer mats, you shan't forget this fortress in a hurry.

WINGING IT

—

Yannick Bolasie

Photography by Amy Maidment

Yannick Bolasie takes time out from putting Premier League defenders on their backsides to meet us at his very first football club and talk about his rise to the top with Crystal Palace.

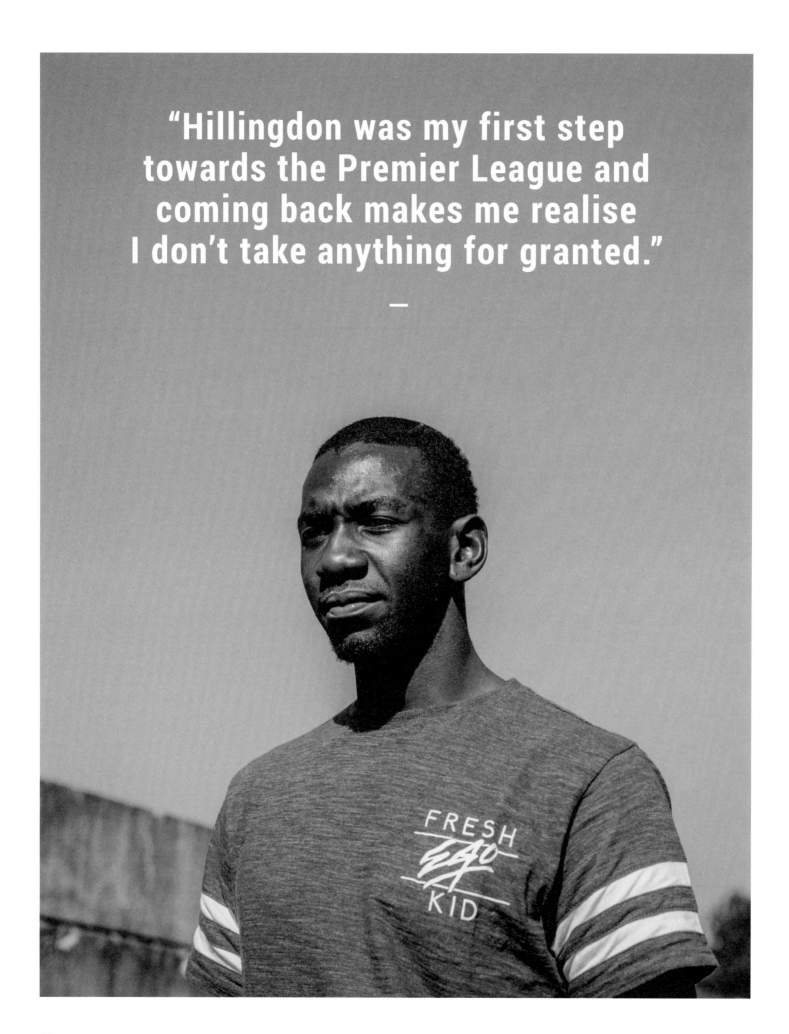

"Hillingdon was my first step towards the Premier League and coming back makes me realise I don't take anything for granted."

—

Yannick Bolasie's route to the Premier League was an unconventional one. Meandering his way through non-league and football league, via a season in Malta, Bolasie finally arrived at England's Promised Land with Crystal Palace. And he wasted no time unpacking his treasure chest of tricks and flicks that have captivated fans of the Premier League. We arranged to meet Bolasie at the place where it all began for him: Hillingdon Borough FC in West London, twenty miles and eight leagues away from Selhurst Park.

"It brings back a lot of memories coming here, you know, seeing people that I remember. Hillingdon was my first step towards the Premier League and coming back makes me realise I don't take anything for granted. When I looked at Hillingdon Borough at the time, their main stadium was actually decent. Flat pitch, you could run with the ball, it was good. Away games were harder – the likes of Didcot, Harrow Borough and Wealdstone. The pitches were on slopes. I didn't know any better, really. I just enjoyed my football at the time."

You frequently hear the phrase "enjoying the game" but Bolasie is a player that truly looks in his element when the ball lands at his feet, and that's when the real fun begins. He'll stand the full back up before turning him inside out, much to the excitement and amusement of the Selhurst Park faithful. It's pure playground football, on the most sophisticated school playing field. And, more importantly, it's entertaining, not to mention effective.

As we look out across the Hillingdon Borough pitch, we ask Bolasie how he's managed hopping up the football ladder at such pace and the changes that brings. "It's the tempo of the game that changes a lot as you come up through the leagues. It's more high intensity the lower you go, whereas the Premier League is a lot more controlled. The Premier League is high intensity in different ways, like when you lose the ball in certain places it can be really dangerous because the other team can score just like that, whereas at lower levels you might get away with it."

"My lifestyle and the way I conduct myself has changed massively over the years too; I'm more professional now. When I [think] back to playing here ... I'd just get off the train and run straight onto the pitch and play football – there was no warm up back then!"

Just four years ago Bolasie was struggling to hold down a position at Bristol City, as managers tried to tame his creativity in favour of a more solid team performance. "It's strange, because when I looked at my situation at the age of 22 it looked like I was never going to get to the Premier League because I was in and out of the Bristol City team. It was hard because the way I like to play wasn't the way I was playing when I was getting the chance. I thought I'd need at least another two seasons of playing regularly before getting picked up, but obviously I moved to Palace, which was a fresh start for me, and luckily got promoted to the Premier League in my first season with the club. Now I'm 25 and playing at the top level so I'm buzzing to be at the stage where I'm at."

The Premier League is more demanding on the body than ever before, and as the game has evolved players have had to carve themselves into finely tuned athletes in order to compete. Bolasie has worked hard to improve his physique since his arrival on the Premier League scene and now he's reaping the rewards. "A few years ago I got my own personal physio to help improve my strength, speed and power. I've become a different athlete. Whereas before I don't think I had enough speed to run up and down the pitch as a winger, now I know I'm in a better physical condition than most players I come up against."

Bolasie's style of football entices defenders to double up on him and moves them out of position, which ultimately benefits his attacking teammates. This perhaps explains why he's involved in so many goals but is rarely the man on the scoresheet. "At Palace I'm trying to rediscover that goalscoring form and get into better positions. My first goal in the Premier League was a really important one. I needed that; it took a lot of pressure off my shoulders. I know I'll get back in amongst the goals so I'm not going to try and force it – I'm not going to change my game for anyone."

Bolasie performs best when the shackles are off, and that's exactly what he's encouraged to do at Palace: create. "As a winger you've got to have that confidence that you can beat your man. That feeling has got to be with me every time I go out onto the pitch. You prepare yourself mentally before a match for those challenges, and you know the player you're going to be playing against is going to win some battles. I look forward to those types of challenges. There's a lot of defenders that are tough to play against – Bacary Sagna, Nathaniel Clyne, Luke Shaw – but that's the Premier League. You're playing against the best of the best."

Bolasie has reached a stage in his career now where the crowd are expectant. Supporters know what he is capable of and Bolasie is the type of player that will naturally have the odd off day due to his risk-taking style of football. He's the type of player a team will look to when things aren't going their way – the player that can provide a spark of magic by taking matters into his own hands to win a game.

Crystal Palace boast two players that can turn a game on its head with one piece of skill. Wilfried Zaha adds another dimension to the Palace front line, and competition is fierce between the two tricksters. "We try and nutmeg each other every day. I nutmegged him recently before I went off for the international break – he was angry about that but he's got me a couple of times to be fair! A lot of the training sessions are high concentration, so it's good to bring some fun into it when we can."

Some players have to be in the zone and get angry before a game, but the topic of fun is one that Bolasie keeps coming back to. "When I go to football, I go there to enjoy it. If I'm enjoying it then I know I'm going to play well. Every time I've played with a smile on my face, that's when I've had my best games. We've got a lot of players who are exciting to watch and we don't hold back. When we play against big teams we like to have a go at them."

"I'd just get off the train and run straight onto the pitch and play – there was no warm up."

—

Step one: Yannick Bolasie reflects on his time playing in the Southern League First Division SouthWest with Hillingdon Borough.

Back to the start: Bolasie returns to the Middlesex Stadium where he'd regularly play in front of crowds of under one hundred.

For Bolasie, music and the mic has always been another avenue for creativity. With an unwavering passion for music, he grew up rhyming, and today is known as much for his MCing as he is for his dazzling runs. "When I was younger, music and MCing is all that I was doing. It all started back in my school days – back then it was either music or football to be honest. We used to have these circles where everyone would make their own lyrics and we'd have class-against-class battles. I wasn't too good at it, but I was always determined to get better. It took me a while to be honest – I used to go to my friend's house and sit there, trying to get my flow and writing bars. Eventually I got better, and then all of a sudden I made it in football. Nowadays I listen to a lot of UK artists, people like Ratlin and Giggs. I like the Americans but I prefer to keep it UK."

Creative in the way he plays the game and creative in what he plays the game in. Exciting, pacey attackers of Bolasie's ability in the Premier League are offered boot contracts and sign them immediately. They see it as free boots and another paycheque. Human mannequins – easy money for some. Bolasie has been offered a boot contract by numerous brands, but like his on-pitch mentality, he can't be restricted. He's laced up limited editions and various throwbacks from his ever-growing collection. "I've kept a lot of boots since the start of my career – I've got the Mercurial I and II so I go back a long way to be honest! It feels weird putting the old ones on now. I was wearing one of my old Vapors in the Championship two seasons ago and they were really comfortable to be fair."

"I've always liked to buy my own boots – it's just been that way since I was young. I like to spend a lot of time breaking boots in, because they have to feel like a sock before I wear them properly on game day. At the moment I'm wearing my Nike's [Mercurial Superfly IV], but I'm also breaking in the Under Armours [SpeedForm], the Umbros [Velocita], and the new adidas boots. I've got so many that I have to get some of the youth boys that are my size to break in a lot for me! I wear whatever I feel comfortable with – I don't really care about getting a boot deal. This way I can do anything I want; it's much better for me." You can't cage creativity, no matter what form it comes in.

THESE STREETS

—

Wilfried Zaha

Photography by Amy Maidment

Wilfried Zaha – a proud South Londoner – has risen from the playground to the Premier League with Crystal Palace. Back at the place he calls "home" and more determined than ever.

Zaha wears Nike Ignite MidLayer
with Nike Duro Reflect ball.

The old stereotypes about South London – a cultural black hole where cab drivers would never venture – are in the past. Nowadays it's more than just the rap music that's making noise this side of the river. The area is a hotbed of raw football talent that's punching its way to the top of the English game. Wilfried Zaha – a proud South Londoner – has risen from the playground to the Premier League with Crystal Palace. Now, with his ill-fated stint at Manchester United behind him, he's back where he calls "home" and more determined than ever.

Born in the Ivory Coast, Zaha moved with his family, including his eight siblings, to Thornton Heath in the London Borough of Croydon, where he would learn his football on the streets. "I came from the Ivory Coast when I was just four years old, so South London is literally all I know. We all lived in a three-bedroomed house I shared with my brothers. It was nice as we were always together, we did everything – we still have a strong bond today. When I started playing football my family had nothing so it's important for me to not forget where I came from. It keeps you grounded, being brought up on these streets and seeing the things you see here – you know, it can still be rough but it's not rough like it was when we were young."

Despite its perceived and often unjustified reputation for crime and gang culture, a combination of regeneration on the South Bank, landmark new developments and improving infrastructure means South London is moving on from its grimy past. "It's portrayed as such a rough place, so when you make it from here people are proud. As soon as people hear 'South London' they just write it off and don't want to know, but now some of today's best footballers and musicians are coming out of here."

"I know a lot of musicians who have made it from here – guys like Stormzy and Krept and Konan. Those guys are my friends so I try to follow them as much as I can and support their music. I'm always keeping my ear to the ground to see what new noises are coming out of South London. Whether it's through football or music, we need to let people know that it's not all that bad."

We're meeting the 22-year-old at a concrete court inside Kennington Park, the type where he would meet regularly as a youngster for pick-up games with his friends, playing football for hours against twenty kids and developing his sixth sense for beating a man. "When I was younger I used to have so much time on my hands, I'd play football all day every day. In Croydon I'd literally play games all the time on concrete pitches like this."

"This is so familiar to me, I'd spend hours just doing tricks in cages like this." Zaha joined Palace as a schoolboy at the age of 12 and quickly rose to prominence with his natural ability and flair. "My parents were always very strict with me from an early age. Even when I was 17 my curfew was 7pm. It was tough because my friends would be out partying and having fun. My parents helped me look at the bigger picture though – they knew how much I wanted it."

"We didn't have much money to go around the family, so when it came to my boots I just wore anything I could get my hands on and whatever my parents could afford. I remember once I trained in an old pair of trainers because I didn't have any boots. Back then though I never really cared, just the fact that I was playing football was enough."

The Palace graduate put in the hours, developing a game built around direct pace and unbelievable skills. "I remember watching the way the Brazilian Ronaldo used to play – he was just ridiculous. Zidane as well, he was another player that I remember watching – I couldn't believe how good he was. I'd watch players like that as a kid and want to be like them. I'd play games at home with my little sister and tell her to try and get the ball off me while I practised tricks and all sorts of different things. If they worked I'd try them in training the next day."

The football hype machine has catapulted countless young talents to stardom before spitting them back out. He has experienced first-hand the pressures that come with being an English football prodigy, but Zaha isn't another dreams to dust story. The skinny kid from South London has been on a journey incomparable to most, from moving away from his homeland to packing his bags and joining one of the world's biggest clubs.

"Going to Manchester United was such a different experience. Manchester is completely different to London so coming back to Palace was like coming back home and coming back to my family." A case of too much too soon perhaps, but now he's back at the club where he made his name, and for the foreseeable future. "After my loan period I was happy to sign back on a permanent deal because it shows that I'm in it for the cause and I want to do the best for the team."

"Fans always buzz off you when you do tricks and beat two or three players – nutmegging someone gives me such a buzz!"

Reunited with the club that know him best, Zaha is back in the first-team picture at Selhurst Park – a place he knows better than anyone. "Going to Selhurst Park now, it still feels like it did when I was a kid. Nothing has changed there – even the chairs are still wooden! The fans, the staff, everything is still the same. It's like a family, I literally know everyone here. The fans are all local people who have a real love for the club. We have people come into the club every day to help and they don't even get paid – they just come in for the love of the club."

It's those same fans who watched on from Selhurst's creaky wooden seats as their most exciting talent left defenders in knots and offered a fresh sense of optimism after periods of genuine dread following the administration threatened season of 2010. "I've gone from watching Palace when they came close to not even being a club any more to playing for them in the Premier League."

Back in the Premier League and back with a spring in his step, Zaha is ready to conquer South London again with the backing of the Holmesdale faithful.

"Fans always buzz off you when you do tricks and beat two or three players – nutmegging someone gives me such a buzz! I know not to let the crowd hype me up too much though because then I'll get carried away. They love the trickery but you need to make sure there's an end product to it. You can do tricks all day long but if you're not adding an end product, what's the point?"

"If I start a game off with a trick that works, I know I'm going to have a good game. Defenders don't like being mugged off though. I remember one time when we were playing against Southampton, I did a trick against this defender and tried to waste time. He ended up taking me out and told me not to disrespect him. I thought, I don't even know you so why would I disrespect you!"

A player that thrives on confidence, the arrival of Alan Pardew in SE25 has helped rebuild Zaha's self-belief on the football pitch, encouraging him to break free and rediscover the sense of professional invincibility that left defenders dizzy. "When he arrived we weren't in the best position but he came in and changed our whole mentality and gave players including myself a lot of belief. I remember when I was at Manchester United and we were playing Newcastle, he shook my hand and wished me good luck just before I was about to come on in the second half. From then I knew he was a good guy."

"When you used to think of Palace, you'd think they're a team that just park the bus. As soon as the gaffer came in he told us to stop fixating on the defensive side. We've always had players who've got skill and pace – players like myself and Yannick (Bolasie) – so he encouraged us to express ourselves a lot more. Personally for me he gave me a lot of confidence – he tells me not to play with any pressure and just play my own game."

"In training it's always me and Yannick who are trying to out-do each other with tricks. He does some really random things though – did you see against Liverpool when he swept the ground with his hands before running off with the ball? He's a funny guy."

Zaha wears Nike
Ignite MidLayer, Tech
Fleece Pant and Air
Max 90 Ultra

"I play FIFA a lot so when I was looking at the FIFA16 trailer I saw him doing his trick next to Neymar and Ronaldo! I messaged him straight away to see if he knew he was on it; he didn't but he was buzzing when I told him."

The tricks have evolved, as have the demanding responsibilities that come with being a Premier League professional. "I have to be so disciplined after training and make sure I'm getting enough rest and eating the right foods – so much of it is about the recovery after a match. If I don't get much rest in between games I get so tired. When you play teams like Manchester City and Chelsea you don't get the ball so you have to recover well after matches like that."

"When you're young you just play for yourself, but now it's very different. I'm part of something and I'm working for a team. No matter how many times I play I still get butterflies and feel nervous before a game, but as soon as I start playing I'm fine. It's a different kind of enjoyment compared to when I was younger, but I still feel the same high when the team wins a game."

His best feeling in a Palace shirt? We should have known. "I'll never forget scoring two goals against Brighton at the Amex. That was the best feeling ever because their fans hated me for some reason, I don't know why! I got so much abuse from them throughout the game, so being the person to score two goals and get us to the final was the best feeling. I was buzzing that night."

After two years away from the Eagles, Zaha is back in the red and blue and soaring once again, ready to create more history with the club that raised him and ready to show anyone who had written him off how wrong they were.

Bold: The "Chilling Red/Bright
Crimson/White" Nike MagistaX
Proximo headlines the winter
'15 FootballX updates

AFTER DARK

—

Nike FootballX & Night Rising

Nike light up floodlit football season with two collections that capture the electric atmosphere of Champions League nights and the crisp, cold air of five-a-side football. Using the black canvas of the empty night sky the 'Night Rising' replica offering and the latest FootballX updates creep out from under the cover of darkness this winter.

Top Nike MercurialX Proximo
"Metallic Gold Grain/Black"

Below Nike HypervenomX Proximo
"Black/Chilling Red"

PSG infuse the City of Light with
a distinct, dark aesthetic.

Inter's European
third shirt goes for
the bold approach.

Manchester City's third
shirt, inspired by the kit
worn in the famous '99
playoff final victory.

Barcelona's European third shirt
receives an electric shade of blue.

IN AMONGST
THE MADNESS

—

From the touchline at NYCFC

Photography by NYCFC / Nathan Congleton

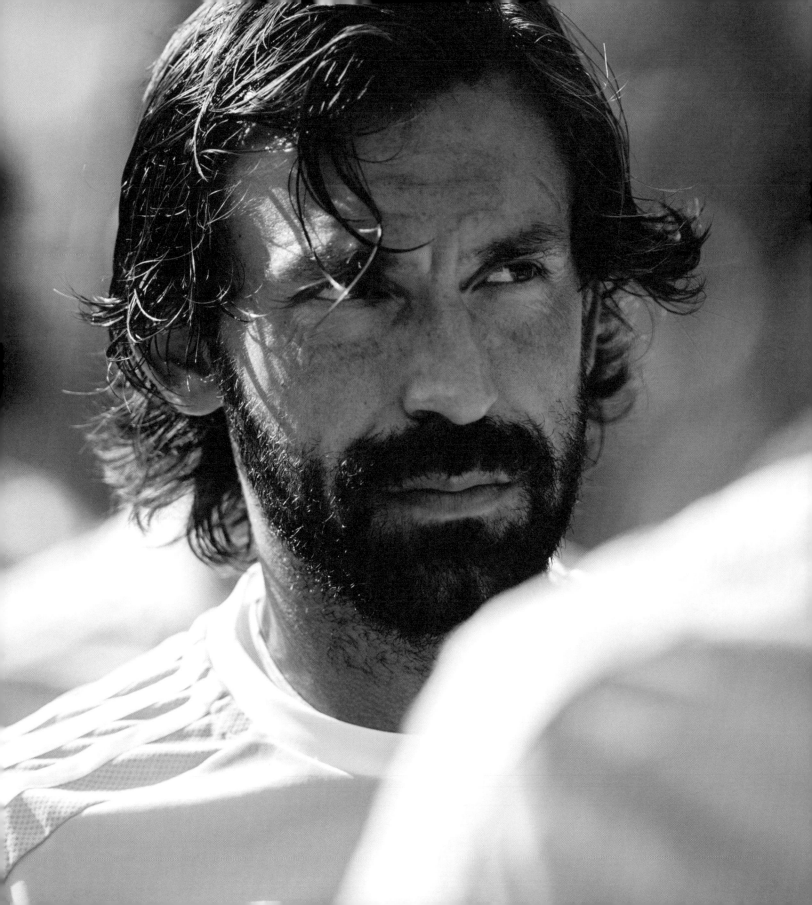

Since the arrival of NYCFC, the work of club photographer Nathan Congleton has established a new benchmark in football photography. Mixing the art of the game with the culture of the chaos, we took five to catch up on his obtuse angle of sight as his camera ushers some of the greats onto fresh football soil.

You have been in the pulpit, as it were, with some of the greatest, most iconic players to have descended on NYC. The likes of Pirlo, Villa and Kaka – how would you describe their presence?

I can definitely tell a difference in the way they carry themselves as opposed to the younger, home-grown generation of players in the league. They have a swagger about them, but they know it's not all about them. It's a team effort and each of them would tell you that.

You've seen them in those almost haunting unique second before they go onto the pitch. What are those moments like?

They are mostly quiet. It's not a loud environment and everyone seems focused on the next 90 minutes, getting down to business. I would be nervous, but they seem so confident in their ability and each other. It's a very 'together' atmosphere.

Seeing the influx of fans, how has the support changed in and around NYC as well as Yankee Stadium? Can you sense that this is more than a passing phase?

New York is all football. If someone told you 5 years ago that 30,000 people would buy a ticket to watch a domestic league game in Yankee Stadium, it may have just sounded like a very ambitious idea, or a crazy one. But it happens week in and week out and the atmosphere surrounding it only goes on to prove that it's not a passing phase at all. It's here to stay and has only gained support as the season has gone on. I think there are around 19,000 founding members in this inaugural season - that's loyalty.

How do you make a player feel at ease when they know there are photos being taken of them?

There has to be a ton of trust involved. As a photographer, it's my job to not only make the person in front of me look as good as possible, but to also notice when they need some space. When I take a photo where everything looks good, but isn't flattering to the player, the image gets trashed for ever because the last thing anyone wants is to look bad in a shot that will make the rounds on social media for ages. My number one priority is to protect the image of the players, while providing usable content to the club.

There is a natural elevation of athletes; we put them on a pedestal, a spotlight that takes them to immortal levels. Do you think you've seen the 'normal' side of football players?

I think footballers and other professional athletes are just as normal as the rest of us. They all enjoy taking their kids to the park, going to the movies or having a nice dinner in a restaurant. I've noticed how kind and well-mannered everyone is. The first day I met Pirlo, he walked in the room and shook everyone's hand and said hello to each person individually, that really stuck with me.

There is an aura around Andrea Pirlo, is it true that there is no party without a Pirlo? What have you seen him add to the NY scene that wasn't there previously?

The party was waiting for them to arrive, the additions of Pirlo and Frank Lampard have elevated that party feeling even more. The feeling is so big, the element of excitement is buzzing before the match even starts. When I arrive 3 hours early, there are people waiting outside to catch a glimpse of our players coming to work.

From your own professional side of things, what's it like being able to capture one of the all-time greats at such close proximity?

It's a privilege for me honestly. I think everyone on the side line who has a media credential and knows a thing or two about the illustrious career that Pirlo has under his belt can't help but lose focus and just simply watch him play from time to time. Sometimes I expect him to go a certain way in a one-on-one situation, but he spins out of the challenge in his own way. I love being surprised by him.

You have witnessed his abilities behind closed doors during training sessions – what moments have made you think, "Wow, this guy is on another level"?

His confidence. In a game or training session, no defender makes him nervous. He just seems to not have a panic button installed in him at all and always finds a way out of sticky situations. It's clear that the guy who was the best in Italy is now the best in the United States. He just does everything better.

What players have you been genuinely awestruck by? What is it about them that separates them from the rest?

I don't get awestruck like I used to, but It's hard to pretend I don't get nervous around Andrea Pirlo and David Villa or Lampard. They are all such unique and special figures in football and I know how good they are and what they mean to the sport and the culture surrounding it. With Pirlo, he's just so cool and recognisable. With the captain, I think of all the times he terrorised teams in La Liga and on the world stage – he's broken a lot of hearts and brought tears of joy at the same time. I often think about how they felt as they lifted the World Cup over their heads in moments of pure glory not only for themselves, but for the countries they represent. It's an incredible opportunity to say hello to them as they arrive at the stadium and make their way to the locker room. That is my favourite part of the day. As for separating them from the rest, I'm not sure that in terms of excitement it is only about the international superstars. Look at the rookie Poku. Every game that he isn't on the field I hear "We Want Pokuuu!" out of every corner of the stadium, and it's not a few shouts here and there. It's everyone in unison, loud and proud. He's won their hearts and trust and it's been incredible to see his work ethic.

Finally, what would you say has been your NYCFC photographic highlight so far?

Easy question. Saturday night at home vs San Jose – the team just ran things in the second half. It's like a switch was flipped and there it was, the engine was roaring and we looked good. Ned Grabavoy scored a brace in quick fashion and gave us a 2-0 lead. In comes Angelino and no sooner does he put one on a plate for Villa in the middle of the box, the captain elevated and scored a peach of a header. Opposite side of the net – it was perfect. Until then, I've been frustrated and had some bad luck getting shots of our captain and his goal celebrations, but that night I was in the right position and he gave me a couple of my favourite shots all season. As he was walking away back to the centre circle, I leaned back against the dugout and let out a sigh of relief – finally.

"Nathan has a lot of gratitude to NYCFC and Manchester City photographer Sharon Latham who serves as creative inspiration for him."

"It's clear that the guy who was the best in Italy is now the best in the United States. He just does everything better."

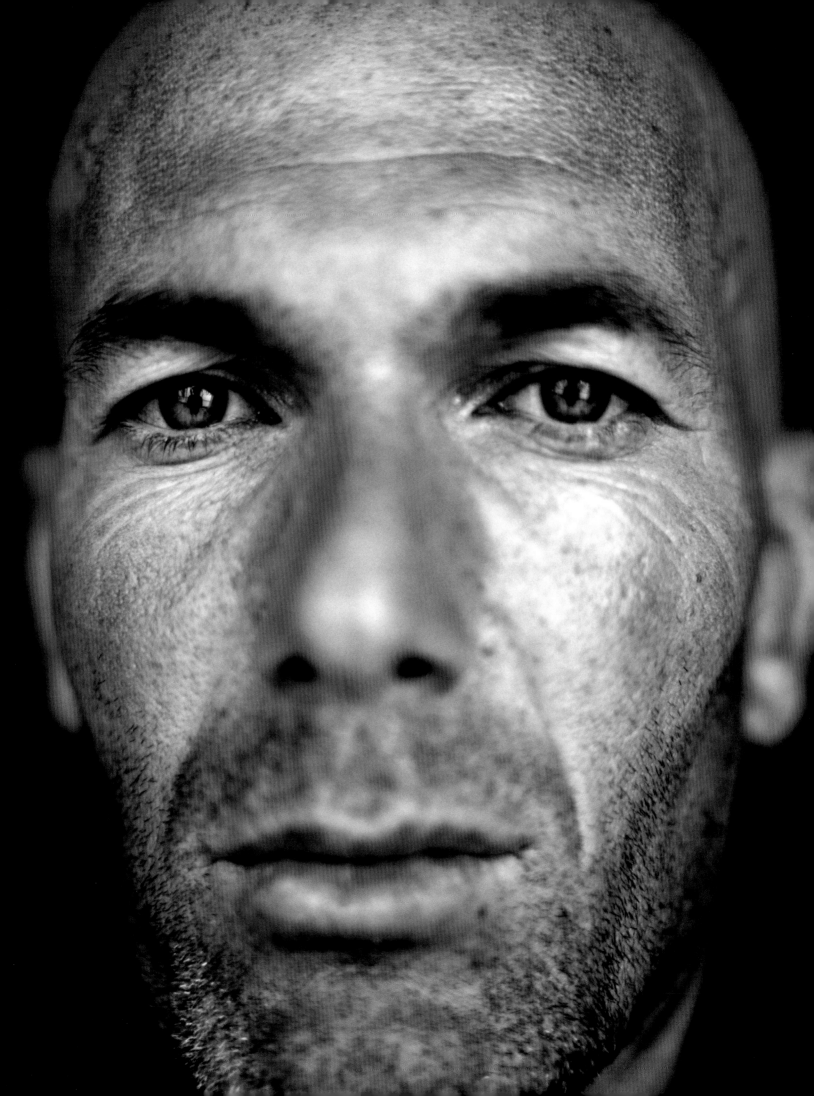

THE
MASTER

—

Zinedine Zidane

Photography by Tom Johnson

Managers built teams around him. Every position, formation and strategy was created to maximise his time on the ball and influence on the game. As Zlatan Ibrahimović accurately observed, "when he stepped onto the pitch the ten other guys suddenly got better." He was told to play his own game, no further instructions were needed. He channelled his anger and aggression into winning trophies and achieving legendary status.

A maverick is defined as 'an unorthodox or independent-minded person' but that definition goes far deeper when describing one Zinedine Zidane. The greatest player of his generation with the ability to single-handedly win games and dictate the pace a of match, he's arguably the most complete midfielder of all time.

There's a real mystique around those bold 'ZZ' initials, the perfect identity to make an impact. The man was destined to stand out and the media took a firm grasp of the double 'Z' to elevate his profile further, not that he needed any help making a mark on the game. Nicknamed 'Zizou', Zidane was born from Algerian descent and that heritage influenced his middle name, Yazid. "I had always been called Yazid by everyone: my parents, my friends... but now everyone calls me Zinedine. Except for my family at home, to them I'm still Yazid or Yaz."

Growing up in a deprived district of Marseille, young Yazid learned to fight for his success. Opportunity wasn't presented to anyone on a plate and it was on these streets where Zidane's fiery temperament and tough mentality was forged.

"Being raised in La Castellane had a huge impact on me because I had to grow up quickly and stand up for myself. In the neighbourhood I had to protect myself, even though I had my friends and brothers around me. I am a very different person today to who I was then. Today I am a calm and laid back person, all the more since I've had kids, but when I was younger I was very boisterous. That was my personality then and I needed that, not to survive, but to impose myself, to make my own way."

"I knew what I wanted: to play football and I did what I had to do to play football. Every day I was outside playing, trying to get better and better. The neighbourhood allowed me to develop this fighting spirit." Only the strongest prevailed in La Castellane, a neighbourhood notorious for crime and unemployment where prospective footballers had to be selfish to succeed. Train hard or be left behind.

Zidane's hunger and desire were key traits throughout a playing career that saw him enter each game with a must-win mentality. No player had a God-given right to win a game of football, each game was a level playing field where work-rate would out-perform talent, although Zidane had an abundance of both.

"I had friends who were very talented but not as hardworking and assiduous at training as I was. They were less passionate about football than I was. I often think of them and they might have been very gifted but I had this thirst for getting better and improving and they gave up football while I managed to make a career out of it."

Zidane wearing the adidas Y-3 Softshell
Bomber from the adidas Y-3 AW15 collection,
available at www.y-3.com

Marseille injects a grit and fearless approach into the blood of its footballers and that blood never took much provocation to bring it to the boil. Eric Cantona was a fine example of another player from Marseille with a tough exterior that would hold his own and often seek out confrontation rather than stepping away from it.

On the pitch Zidane used football as an outlet to release an inner rage. He admits he was angry as a young player and that temper resulted in a double-digit red card count over the course of his career, some highlighted more than others.

Hard and uncompromising, he wouldn't take any prisoners on the pitch, making him all the more intimidating for opponents. Shying away from tackles or getting bullied wasn't part of his character but off the field it was a different story and the reason he identified with Enzo Francescoli - an attacking midfielder who Zidane refers to as his biggest idol and a player he could relate to.

"Francescoli inspired me. He was a stylish player. He was beautiful when he played. That's the perfect definition of him: he was a beautiful player. We never saw or heard much about him outside of the field, he was very discreet. But once he stepped out on the field he was beautiful."

At a time when other Marseille team-mates were huge stars who enjoyed their celebrity status and the hedonistic distractions the city offered, Francescoli kept a low profile and, like Zidane, remained focused on his football.

"What really struck me at the time was his ball control" says Zizou, touching on the Uruguayan's talents. "When you're young and admire someone there is always one characteristic feature that stands out, and for me it was his ball control abilities."

The first encounter with his idol on the pitch left a lasting impression on the young Frenchman. "I had the opportunity to play against him. I told him what I liked about his play, and he told me that in his opinion, the student had surpassed the teacher. That went straight to my heart because every time I touched the ball, every single move I did, I wanted to look like him."

It's becoming increasingly rare for elite level footballers to stay out of the public eye. Nowadays players have their own social media accounts to keep fans up-to-date and, ultimately make them more marketable for sponsors. Every move is documented by the club and that's a new trend for players from Zidane and Francescoli's era. On the pitch though, he points towards a different type of change - intensity.

"The game goes much faster on the field. But what has changed the most in today's football is the importance of communication, celebrity, all that is said about footballers, every minute. Today's footballers don't have time for themselves, moments when they can hide away and keep silent. That doesn't exist anymore. One must accept to live with that. But to be honest I think most footballers are OK with that as they grew up in this new world, with mobile phones, in that era where everything goes fast. They are products of their time. That's a major difference for me: we know everything about everyone."

Zidane saved all his intensity for the pitch, that was how he wanted to be judged, by what he left on it after 90 minutes of football. Making himself into a brand or celebrity wasn't important, he cared for the game only.

"I've always had a strong personality. That's who I was on the field but then very discreet outside. I would keep silent and spend time with my family. It totally suited me and I wouldn't change a thing to what I did then because I expressed myself on the field but then I kept calm outside. That was a good compromise."

In his younger days Zidane was a loose cannon with a short fuse. More experienced players found easy ways of lighting that fuse and triggering a reaction. However, as he grew up he learnt to control his temper and for that he thanks his family.

"My parents and siblings taught me those values of respect, hard-work and steadiness. My wife later played that role too. She's the one who helped me, stayed by my side and gave me great advice in complicated times. Because she has a very strong personality like I have it was great: I've listened to her advice very carefully. Thanks to her I never lost my mind."

The ability to harness the aggression and intensity inside him went a long way to establishing Zidane as one of the greatest players of all-time. Such traits were part of his personality, shaped by his experiences on the streets of the southern port city and can't be easily taught.

An aggression and a determination to be the best is what makes the best. "I haven't always been able to channel it, but that was part of my personality, part of my life. I've had ups and downs, nevertheless, I needed that aggressiveness on the field to express myself. I knew I had great qualities but that is not always enough. A lot of players today have talent but if they don't express their own personality, their true character on the field, they won't go anywhere. It's never been truer than today: there are a lot of excellent players around, so in the end that's what will make a real difference: personality."

The feisty young Frenchman that was tearing up Europe in the 1990's has become more laid back now his playing days are over. The Zinedine Zidane that sits in front of us is a manager, simultaneously passing on his wisdom and picking it up at Real Madrid Castilla, the club's second string side made up of players under the age of 25.

"When I was younger I was very boisterous. That was my personality then and I needed that, not to survive, but to impose myself, to make my own way."

The qualities required of a manager are of course different and Zidane had to make that transformation before swapping the shorts and shirt for the suit. "Between 2006 and 2015 I've done a lot of work on myself. When I put an end to my career in 2006 I decided to be calmer and focus on my family. But when you decide to go back to business as I do today, as a coach, you must show your claws again." The fire is back in his belly and he's already educating his young squad even though his own playing talents were somewhat unteachable.

"The one piece of advice I always give to football players is that there are only two key ingredients to getting better: keep focused and bring intensity to your play. Those are the two things that allow a player to improve. A player with talent and qualities can have a great career if he adds these two ingredients. Then, hard work, training and respect are important too. I sometimes hear that today's young players are different from their elders, that they lack respect but it's not true. Players are a reflection of their coach's behaviour. They react and play accordingly to the morals he's given them. That's why I show my claws again today; players need to be firmly shown the right direction."

"It's a process of trials and mistakes but if I make mistakes it's not that important because I am still learning too. Being a coach is a totally different job from being a football player. I show my claws again because I really want players to understand that through hard work and steadiness, focus and intensity they will get better. I sincerely believe in that."

There's a real presence about Zidane. He exudes a certain authority just by walking into the room. Not many footballers can do that. When he talks the room is silent, it feels as if every word he speaks is a life lesson, so we can only imagine the respect he has in the Castilla changing room surrounded by players who grew up worshipping him and are now desperate to add even the smallest influence of their idol to their own game.

> I often compare adidas to a football club: to be number one a club needs the best players, the best crew, and in a similar way adidas employs the best people around, at every level. It shows in the quality of their products."

When Zidane was the same age as his Castilla squad he was already packing his bags for Juventus, having made a name for himself in his home country with Cannes and Bordeaux. Playing in multiple countries and being immersed in multiple cultures helps any individual grow. It was in Italy where Zidane matured and took his talents to the next level by playing in what was the greatest league in Europe at the time.

"To put it simply, moving to Italy was a milestone in my career. I had received a great training in France, but when I became a professional player and joined a club I realised that winning was not always the most important thing. In Italy however, even during a friendly match with nothing at stake, we had to win. In Italy I was taught to develop a true winning spirit. I went to Italy in 1996, when Italian football was absolutely beautiful, I joined a club with great players so I had to be excellent too. I had to show my personality. I was the young Frenchie, away from home for the first time ever. Italians taught me what the winning spirit is."

This 'young Frenchie' was joining a Juventus team that had previously been masterminded by Michel Platini. There were big shoes to fill in Turin but Zidane is his own man and he was never going to try on Platini's. He'd brought his own with him and they were already full of talent and attitude. "Replacing Platini never crossed my mind. People mentioned his name though, because when I joined I played as number ten and had been selected in the French national team. I just wanted to be a good player. Italians did compare us, inevitably but I never really cared and never felt any pressure about it."

In the era when Zidane joined Juventus, several artists and magicians were already performing tricks and casting their spell in Serie A, but Zidane calls out Paolo Maldini as the most unique. "I admired several players such as Baggio, but to me the ultimate football player, the one who embodied football at its best and who was an absolute role model, was Maldini. I see professional football as a whole - what counts is not only the attitude of the player on the field but also outside, how he reacts, how he speaks. Maldini had a lot of class. He was a great example."

Maldini, like Zidane, was a gentleman off the pitch but a warrior on it. Both players knew that rewards in football come solely from working hard and that's a message Zidane now passes on to the players under his watch at Castilla. "I tell my players to love what they do keeping in mind that it only lasts 15 years. I often remind my team, made up of young players who have barely started playing, that time goes by quickly and things move fast." Zidane the manager is already finding his own analogies and is clearly focused as much on player mentality as he is with coaching technical skills.

"I tell my players to enjoy what they do, to make the best of every single occasion they touch the ball. I often use the comparison with a basketball player. When a basketball player shoots, he puts the ball through the basket with maximum concentration, entirely focused on what he's doing. It is an absolutely beautiful moment. Football players should have exactly the same attitude during a match: they should stay focused and bring the same intensity into every single move, pass or shot. I did just that when I trained to shoot the ball with my left foot. I spent hours after hours shooting balls into a wall and I am now almost a better striker with my left foot than I am with my right foot." (See Champions League Final, 2002.)

That volley against Bayer Leverkusen was the greatest goal ever scored in the history of the competition, a moment of pure technical magic but Zidane references the graft put in beforehand to typify his mentality. "That happens only once in the life of a footballer, that happened to me at the right time but I was able to shoot that ball because of the hard work I had done."

Zidane talks a lot about focus and expressing personality so we question him on which current players demonstrate those qualities. Being involved with Real Madrid meant that there was only one man who was ever going to be referenced here. "Ronaldo" he tells us, shrugging as if it was the easiest question we asked him all afternoon. "He is so focused in every move he makes. He has a true eagerness to be the best and that's simply what he is. That competition between Messi and him is beautiful and very healthy. That explains why they are both at their best. It's beautiful to watch. Ronaldo scored 300 goals in 288 matches. No one can beat Ronaldo."

With a license to do whatever he wanted, Zidane was a genuine footballing maverick who was at his most dangerous when he had carte blanche to express himself. His directions from the dugout replicate that freedom to experiment and be the match-winner, a tactic surely influenced by the confidence in his own ability as a player. "I teach young footballers to defend when they don't own the ball but feel entirely free to take risks when they have the ball. That's the lesson I give to my players in the team I coach: be defensive when your team doesn't control the ball but then, if you're in the 30, 40 meters area from the opponents goal, that's when you have to be creative and use your imagination. That's the time and situation when players shouldn't feel constrained, they must be left to express themselves." Music to the ears of an attacker.

Over the last two decades Zidane has provided unforgettable moments of unpredictable genius as an adidas player. Only David Beckham is in the same category as Zidane as a priceless brand ambassador. It's a relationship that has flourished and played a pivotal role in installing the adidas Predator as

arguably the greatest football boot of all-time. "I've been working with adidas since 1996 when I joined Juventus." A twenty year relationship is impressive in any walk of life so why has it worked so well for Zizou? "As in any relationship it's a question of trust" he tells us. "I'm always faithful to adidas because they've always been faithful to me. I brought a lot to the brand but they also gave a lot back to me. The fact that we still collaborate even though I put an end to my career ten years ago is proof that we get along very well. Over time people have come and gone at adidas, I've met a lot of different people, but the general politics of the brand have always stayed the same: to care about the athlete's well-being first. That's the feeling I always had and still have today."

"I often compare adidas to a football club: to be number one a club needs the best players, the best crew, and in a similar way adidas employs the best people around, at every level. It shows in the quality of their products."

When we think of Zidane and adidas, one of the first images that springs to mind is the signature golden Predator Absolute worn in the 2006 World Cup Final against Italy and designed by the man himself. "adidas offered to create a boot for me, for the World Cup, in a colourway that I would only wear during the final. I was asked to pick a colour. Gold is my favourite colour so it made sense to me to wear golden boots. I still have that pair of boots at home. Over time I have given away shirts and boots that I have worn. I am a very generous person, a bit too much sometimes! But I have always kept these boots. They're in my closet at home right now. I'll never get rid of them, I'll pass them on to my children as a souvenir of their dad."

As we all know Zidane didn't read the script that adidas had written for that final, but that wouldn't have been in his nature. He was unpredictable, a true maverick. Some say it wasn't the right way for him to retire. It wasn't. It was perfect. His next chapter is still unwritten but Zidane the manager is ready, and as he says, it's time to show his claws again. And those claws are as sharp as ever.

"Between 2006 and 2015 I've done a lot of work on myself. When I put an end to my career in 2006 I decided to be calmer and focus on my family. But when you decide to go back to business as I do today, as a coach, you must show your claws again."

—

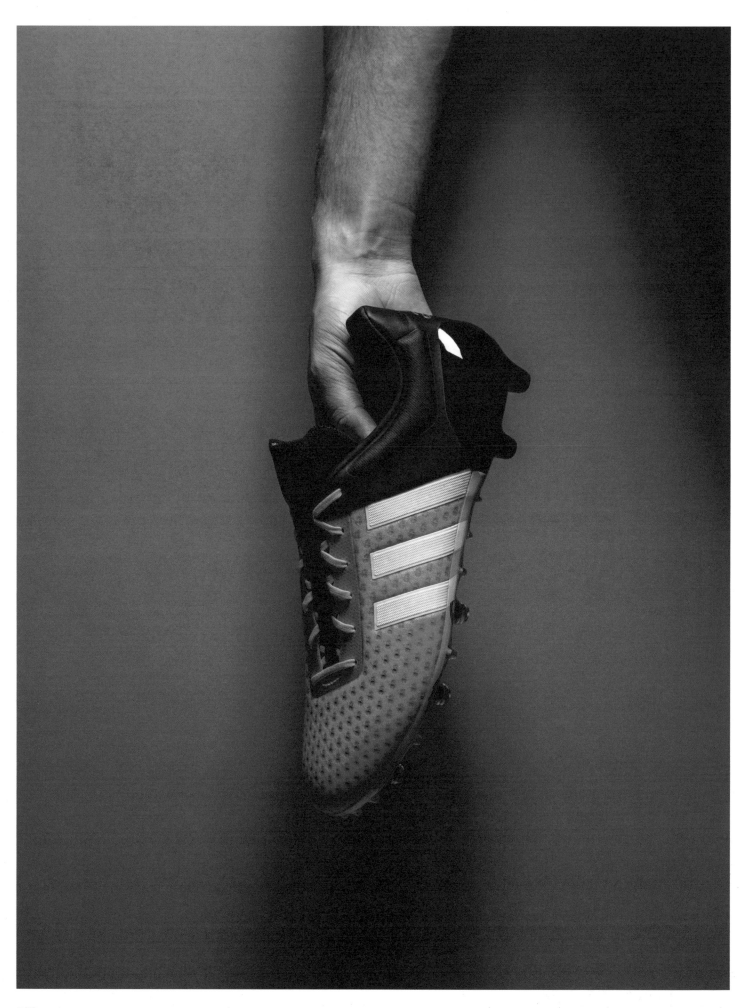

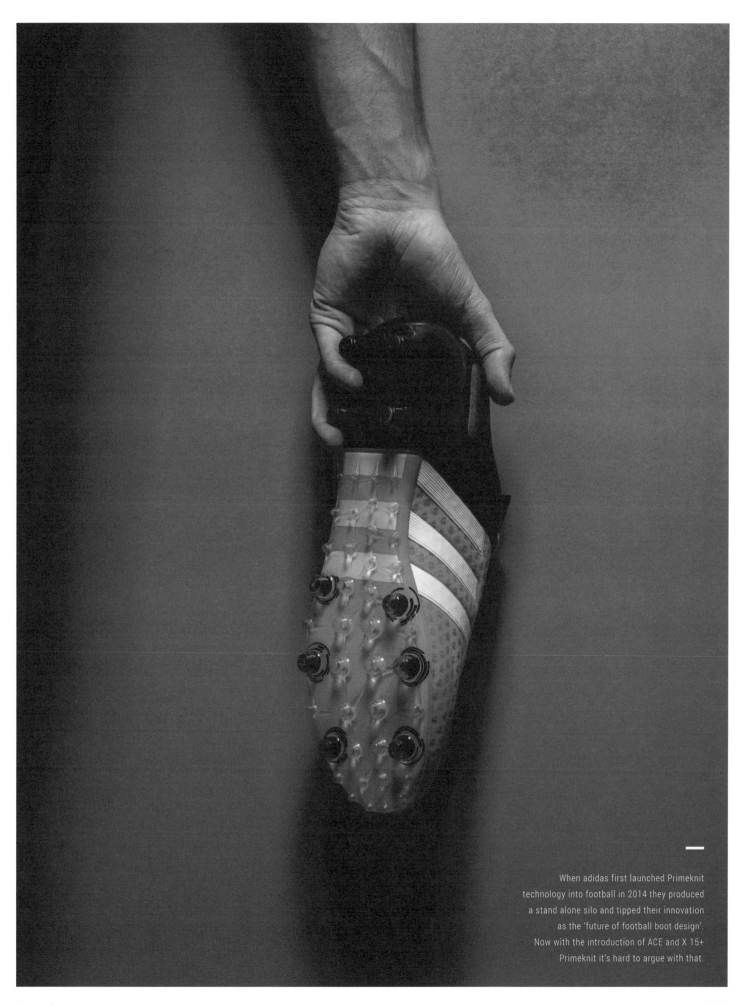

When adidas first launched Primeknit
technology into football in 2014 they produced
a stand alone silo and tipped their innovation
as the 'future of football boot design'.
Now with the introduction of ACE and X 15+
Primeknit it's hard to argue with that.

Comfortable Chaos. After tinkering with
first iterations of the tech, adidas have
combined their latest lightweight silo with
their most advanced materials to create
a line-up that optimises the fearless new
approach of the brand.

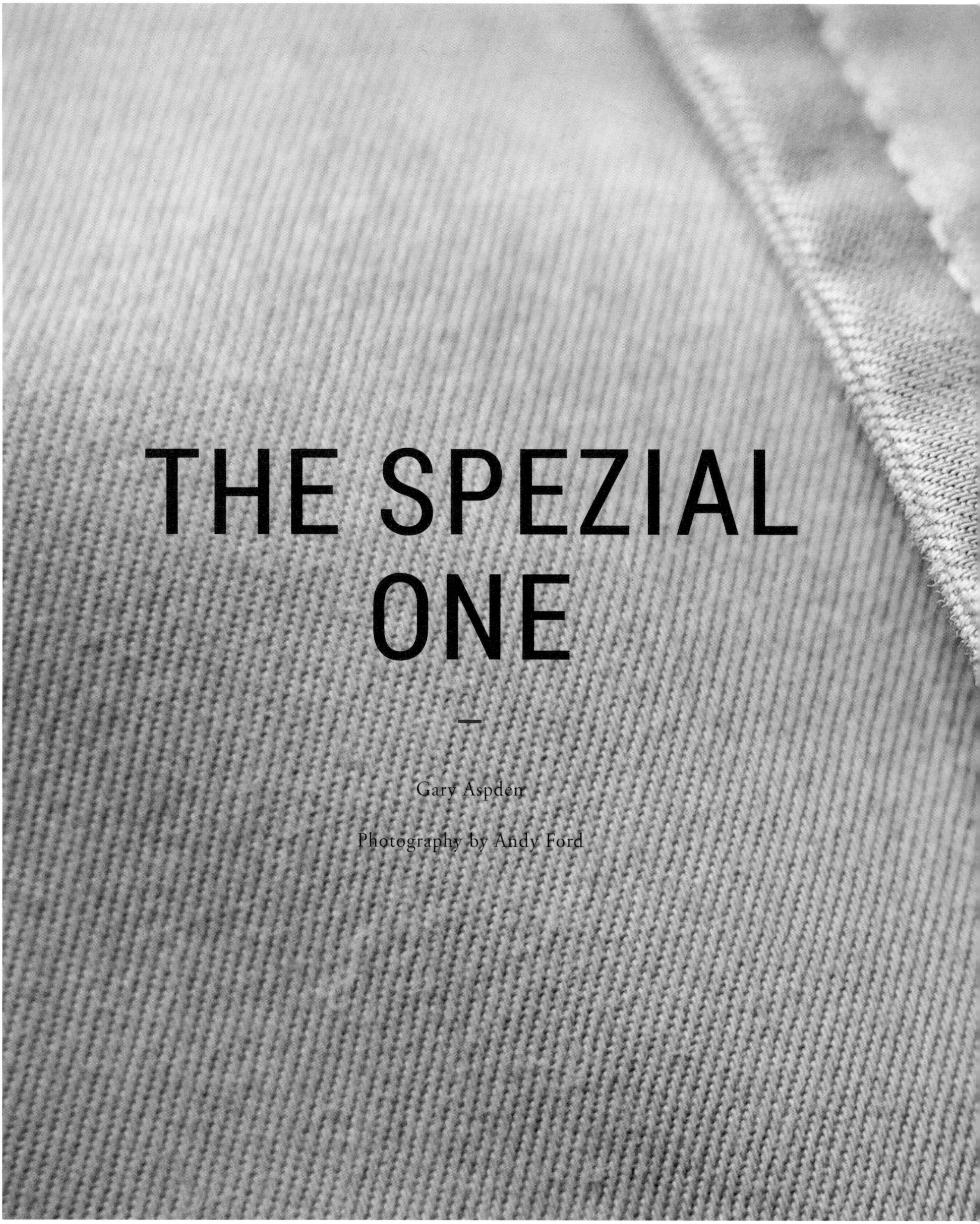

THE SPEZIAL ONE

—

Gary Aspden

Photography by Andy Ford

Football can be a crowded game. With players on the pitch given a small slice of turf to battle over, their room for manoeuvre is limited. In the stands however, the fashion of football is vividly powerful. A visual expression from the lifeblood of the game, trends have captured the passion of football in a way no words could; it is a hotbed for the cultured supporter. Offering a fascinating insight on an undercurrent of creativity that takes in the holy trinity of music, fashion and football, we got an education from a hero in adidas circles, Gary Aspden.

The curator of the adidas Originals x SPEZIAL range, Gary Aspden is a source of great inspiration. From humble beginnings to personable influencer, his roots run deep, to the core of adidas, with a heart in Lancashire. "I grew up in a 2 bedroom terrace house in a town called Darwen near Blackburn. My dad worked in a mill and my mum worked in the markets. My mum used to get stuff from the catalogue because you could pay monthly or whatever. My first pair of branded trainers would have been mid to late 70's and they were adidas Kick." A relationship that started at a young age, football forms a sizable part of his background. With a genuine love for the game, he was infected by its spirit in his formative years. Whether it's jumpers for goalposts or wall markings for crossbars, his sentiment resonates style and taste from a respectful place. "My first boots were Beckenbauer Super and I guess things were very different back then. The Beckenbauer Super's were black with white stripes and red studs and I remember immediately wanting to take the red studs out and replace them with aluminium studs 'cos I didn't want to look flash".

We all have our first major tournament that captured the imagination. For this game changer it was '74, a year in which Franz Beckenbauer lifted the trophy donning those timeless boots. The '78 World Cup was another benchmark in the memory of Aspden "I remember going on holiday to Spain and me and my brother badgered my mum and dad to buy us a Tango football. It was like a local legend, that football, 'cos you couldn't buy it where we lived. We'd literally have kids come and knock on our door and ask if they could see the football. We would all play football every day but the Tango would only come out on special occasions and we'd only play with it on grass."

Moving closer to the pitch, a picture postcard of beautifully British nostalgia goes hand in hand with Gary's early memories of Blackburn Rovers. "I had to take the washing-up bowl out of the sink on Saturday and carry it to Ewood Park and put it by the wall so I could stand on it, on my tip toes, just to be able to see over the top. It rains a lot where I come from and sometimes it would be the longest 90 minutes of my life 'cos I'd be down the front getting soaked".

This was an era of the game that is looked back upon with a wash of memories. Portraits painted through cinema, the tale of poetic and raw football has been told by many. It may well be 'the good old days' for some but Gary speaks honestly about that time. For all the fond memories, there is still a sense of harsh realism as to what football was genuinely like as a kid in the riot.

"I think a lot of people have rose-tinted glasses when it comes to football in the 80's. There were so many things about it that were great; muddy pitches, players dodging dog shit, training on a park just up the road from the ground but there was a dark side to 80's football too. I remember going away to Derby with Blackburn and coming out of the ground and me and a mate of mine got separated from the Blackburn fans. It was pretty terrifying. It was like being behind enemy lines. It was scary. There was something about 80's football that was great but sometimes people don't talk about the nasty right-wing stuff that was going on which I didn't have a lot of time for."

One thing that reigned supreme however was the off-the-pitch style that dressed this era from 1980 onwards. "It was skin-tight jeans, white socks, adidas trainers, Fred Perry t-shirts, Slazenger V-Neck sweaters, lots of burgundy and adidas ST2 waterproof jackets. adidas, Fred Perry etcetera laid the foundations. Right through the 80's it was about constantly trying to keep up with what brands and what looks were coming through next. From Slazenger it went to Pringle and Lyle and Scott to Lacoste. As soon as Lacoste polo shirts arrived, you were finished if you were seen in Fred Perry. As soon as it moved on from something, you would have to discard the other stuff. Then it got into expensive European sportswear, brands like Fila and Sergio Tacchini and what happened was

Right Gary Aspden
stands in stature.
A deep history and
proud wearer of West
German Blousen
Jacket - Part of
the SPEZIAL AW15
collection.

it went from that into European casual brands like Armani, Valentino, Hugo Boss and Marco Polo and, eventually, Stone Island. It just kept evolving. adidas and Lacoste were probably the only two brands that didn't get discarded. With adidas, as the looks were changing, they kept coming out with new ranges and complimented everything that came out."

"It gets attributed as football fashion but it was kind of working class fashion, there were a lot of kids who dressed in those clothes who didn't even go to football. Back then it was all pre-internet so you took your style tips from the youth clubs, the local discos, the football. You took it from what was going on around you, in your environment. Different towns had different takes on this look. You were influenced on what was available around you. There wasn't eBay. You couldn't fake it back then; you were either in it or you weren't."

Fast forward the scene into the 90s and Gary's words portray a world that perhaps would parallel that of Shane Meadows. An easy comparison to make, their careers resemble expressions from experience. They say "write about what you know." In this case it's "articulate your experiences." The SPEZIAL collection is one that visually represents who Gary Aspden is.

"What I've always wanted with Spezial is not to adhere to industry formulas. It needs to be interesting and challenging, it doesn't have the immediacy of a third party collaboration which in many ways makes life much harder cos you've got to build something. I think there's an honesty to it and people sense that, they know that the guy behind it feels about adidas how they feel about adidas."

It's all about authenticity and Aspden is a champion of that. Never one to undermine the intelligence of the audience, he's a consumer of his own curations just as much as the audience. He's lived it, in every sense. Starting college in Preston, his introduction to the world of fashion was through unconventional means. In the late 80's he began studying Fashion Design though the lure of the Hacienda, the exploding rave scene and the cultural trip meant studies went on hold. "I spent more time in Hacienda than I did in college and I dropped out after a year. People talk about "Madchester" because a lot of bands came from that area but there was actually very little going on in Manchester itself after 2am. Most people would migrate up to Blackburn on a Saturday.

"I think a lot of people have rose tinted glasses when it comes to football in the 80's."

—

There were so many empty factories and warehouses so it was a breeding ground for parties. So I watched it go from 30 people in a flat to 10,000 in a warehouse with riot police outside."

With the mid 90's beckoning, Aspden returned to college, this time embarking on a Fashion Promotions course. "I had these two middle age ladies asking me where I'd been for the previous 5 or 6 years."

After ironing out the finer details of being a little older than the typical inductee, he excelled at this point with first class honours. "I started college late so in turn I started my career late. I was doing an internship when I was 27 and going for interviews at fashion labels saying I'd work for free. It all kind of came together in my final year of college. There was a girl who was doing entertainment promotions for adidas who I used to hook up with people I knew from the music industry.

On the back of that she'd give me free trainers, which seemed like a good deal to me as I didn't have a lot of money at the time. She ended up getting the sack and they had all these unfulfilled orders with me as a contact number so adidas rung me up thinking I was some big time music manager. I explained to them that I was student in his final year who was trying to connect this lady with people I knew in the music industry."

Having become so entwined with the music industry, his unique connections and character paved the way for a long-standing career with the brand.

"I believe that what I've done with adidas is much more informed by my experiences as a youth. When I joined adidas I had very deep product knowledge 'cos I grew up with those products and we would beg, borrow and steal to get a new pair of trainers. I came from all that and that gives me an instinct for the brand which has proved to be really valuable."

It's a common factor among those who break away from the norm - possessing qualities that can't necessarily be taught. Raw instinct paired with the correct understanding has proved to be a winning formula. All the while, the involvement of football, fashion and music have been ever-present themes.

The AW15 SPEZIAL collection is a feast of curated culture. From Noel Gallagher to Stormzy, its audience is diverse with an appreciation for a strong look. In rather triumphant fashion, "it glances at the past but doesn't stare at it". Gary Aspden's tenure at the brand has helped position adidas Originals at the very apex of fashion, football and music, establishing it as the powerhouse of cool that it has become. A career born out of passion. Great people attract great people. That's true about Gary and it's evident about SPEZIAL.

Above The launch of the SPEZIAL AW15 collection. Style of the highest order on show – Curated cool.

Middle Providing the soundtrack. The guitar of Bill Ryder-Jones leans patiently.

Top Right Noel Gallagher and
Bobby Gillespie among the crowd.
A whole lot of appreciation all
round for the adidas Originals x
SPEZIAL AW15 collection.

GOALARZA

_

Florencia Galarza

Photography by Nathan Congleton

A new level of football sass, Florencia Galarza picks up the beat on her world that is dominated by the vibrant colour, sounds and style of the beautiful game.

Your relationship with football has been turbulent – can you tell us what the game means to you?

Futbol means a few simple things, beginning with family. From watching endless games as a kid with my grandpa to fighting to win championships with my team, futbol and family have always played a very important role in my life.

On a fast trajectory to the top, your chance at reaching the elite on the pitch was tragically cut short. What happened?

When I was 14 I was scouted to try out for Florida ODP – Olympic Development Program – and made the team for years to follow, as well as having the opportunity to try out for Regionals and the US National pool. I was playing on an elite travel team as the youngest member, which exposed me to an insane level of play.

Unfortunately all the incredible soccer experience and training and prep for my future came to an abrupt and very crushing end. Early in my senior year of high school, we were training for a showcase tournament in North Carolina where I had plans to finalise recruitment talk with the college team I had my heart set on, and SNAP – there goes my ankle. All of it. I was carried off the pitch and that was it for me.

You've returned to the game but from a different angle. How did that come to fruition?

Some people take setbacks as something that can set them back. I took my injury as an opportunity to pivot in my life, have an inflection point, and push me forward to focus on my other loves, which are music, fashion, and art. Getting injured put a harsh end to my trajectory as a young professional or USWNT hopeful but it allowed me the opportunity to move to NYC, attend Fashion Institute of Technology, and contribute to NYC culture.

For the last 10 years in NYC, I worked at places like Nylon Magazine and helped ignite downtown NYC nightlife culture. I was a founding member of the DJ crew 'Been Trill', which led to DJing for Jay-Z and Kanye West in Cannes one summer and then on tour with them, DJing backstage and at after parties during the 'Watch the Throne' tour in Europe. I even did a DJ set on BBC Radio 1 for Benji B. DJing has allowed me to put my stamp on global creative culture, and travel the world. Getting injured might have halted my young soccer career, but it also unlocked a future in global creative culture.

Top Right
Regal cool. PUMA
Kings and Umbro
England shorts. Late
90s gold.

Top Left
Boca flair. All the
attitude, football
sass. Game on.

Left

Italian stripes. AC Milan vintage glory. One hell
of a shirt.

Right

United rebellion. Still enjoying the Umbro
prowess. A 90s pace setter.

Last fall I trained and ran the NYC marathon with Christy Turlington. It was a crazy physical journey that landed me a major life milestone as an athlete and a feature in Harper's Bazaar. Coming off of training so aggressively for 26.2 miles, and motivated by the cultural energy of being in Rio for the World Cup, I realised that I was healthy enough, 10 years after my injury, to enjoy futbol again. I'm now a co-captain of the KITH Bowery Premier League team – and my guys can play. They keep me on my toes!

On the professional side, I recently landed two jobs that were awesome. One was working as an on-camera host for KICK TV during the Copa America and the Women's World Cup, which allowed me to show the soccer community that I know the game for real, with a side of sass! The other is a recurring role as a DJ for The US Soccer Federation. I DJ'd the USWNT's last send-off game before the Women's World Cup (I got to DJ on the sidelines!) and the recent USMNT game versus Brazil.

Your passion for the game is rooted in South American heritage. How would you define football in Argentina?
Futbol in Argentina is wild. In the best way possible. I've seen some grown men cry over an insignificant loss and it's absolutely beautiful. Our country has had its share of problems, which has caused people severe misfortune and crazy struggle, but when it's game day, nothing

else matters. They throw on their club's kit and it's 90 minutes of every emotion ever. I really wish Argentina would win the World Cup. Not just for bragging rights but to fuel our country with positive energy. Futbol is a religion. Ask Pope Francis, he gets it.

New York is rapidly becoming an almighty place to be where football is concerned. Can you feel the swell of the world's greatest language: football?
Absolutely. Last summer the streets of NY were on fire during the World Cup. The bars were packed and the enthusiasm was something I've never seen before in the US. The addition of NYCFC has been major and has turned many people onto soccer. It's really amazing that New Yorkers as well as the rest of the US are really feeling the football fury! Not only are they MLS fans but they are really getting involved with European soccer as well. You'd be surprised how many knowledgeable English Premier League super fans are right here in the US.

The football wardrobe is one of many patterns and cuts. Do you have a favourite kit?
Jorge Campos had the most outrageous goalie kits of all time and I thank him for doing his thing. Jokes aside, I have far too many to narrow it down to one. My personal style never really evolved past 1998 so pretty much all shirts, shorts, warm up kits, haircuts, socks, and soccer balls from back then are my favourites.

STYLE & STEEL

—

John Brayford

Photography by Robbie Jay Barratt

The stereotypical image of a footballer has often been tacky and uncultured, so it's refreshing when a player breaks those stereotypes and possesses an unconventional off-pitch style not normally associated with a footballer. John Brayford is rock 'n' roll football.

"He's not just any full back, he's John Brayford." The words of Sheffield United co-chairman Jim Phipps when questioned on how the League One club could justify spending seven figures on a full back. Brayford was a regular for a Cardiff side knocking on the Premier League door, but dropped a league and took a pay cut to join a club he fell in love with during a resurgent loan spell.

Is football still cool? Many would reference the individualities of players from yesteryear, compare them to the robotic player personalities manufactured from the modern Premier League factory, and argue that football cool has peaked. But if you look in the right places, football cool is still very much alive.

As we stand outside Sheffield United's Bramall Lane stadium, a 2000-reg Mini Cooper rocks up; Brayford steps out under a black fedora hat, complemented by braces, motorcycle jeans and Steve McQueen boots. His look is distinctive – more musician than

footballer – and he describes his style as independent. "If I see something I like then I'm not going to be put off by what people are going to think. I just pick out things from the past and present and go for the gentleman sort of style. I think people take it too far with pink jackets and stuff, but it's not like I go out of my way to make sure I dress differently to everyone else."

"I like Johnny Depp's style, and Serge from Kasabian – people who have an aura about them more than anything. Not necessarily just what they're wearing but the vibe they give off. I get quite a lot of my stuff from 'Noose & Monkey' at the moment. There's this guy down in London who's got some cool clobber too: Joshua Kane. He used to work at Burberry and he's just set up some stuff on his own. He's a bit more wild but he's good."

There's a satisfaction when a player doesn't follow the crowd and ultimately challenges the perception of how a footballer can be interpreted by adding a cultured edge to the game. "I've always been like that. I've never been into tracksuits, but that's just my personal taste. I'm not going to sit here and say

what people should and shouldn't wear. People follow trends too easily, but my friends are similar to me – it's influenced by the people you mix with."

Fashion and music go hand in hand, so it's unsurprising that Brayford controls the decks in the club's gym. "I like Kasabian, and one of the first gigs I went to was Oasis at the Old Trafford Cricket Ground, which was a real awakening into that world. My mate's doing alright at the moment – Ryan Dooley. He used to be in 'All The Young', and we used to travel all across the country with them. I make sure there's a mixture in the gym though: you need stuff for everyone. We can go from Spice Girls to 80's punk, but I try and get stuff that all the lads can have a sing-along to."

"I'm big into Neil Diamond at the moment but I don't know why! I've been listening to 'Forever In Blue Jeans' in the gym and my missus is fed up of me playing it now." It's a track that maybe has more of a meaning to Brayford than he realises, with the opening lyrics, 'Money talks, but it don't sing and dance, and it don't walk.' A real 'money can't buy happiness' message, which relates nicely to his

transfer to the Steel City. Music is an ever-present piece in Brayford's diverse wardrobe, as references to lyrical inspirations are mapped out in tattoos across his arms like an incomplete soundtrack to his life.

His style and throwback attitude have installed him as a fans' favourite in South Yorkshire and we ask him what he puts that down to. "That's such a hard question to answer. I'd like to think it's because they can relate to me – I'll always have a drink with the fans after the game because that's important." It's the human traits that fans appreciate, and that demonstrate the honest, genuine feel of the Football League in comparison with the top division.

"I go up my local pub a couple of times a week – you meet the most interesting people in those sorts of places. I'll stand at the bar on my own and you can speak to anybody: it's brilliant. I don't know if that's the vibe I give off to them but I just love it up here – the people are great. I've just bought a house here and I said to my missus, 'I'm not moving away from this pub.' We were on Rightmove and I set the distance [to] no further than a quarter of a mile from the pub!"

As we make our way around the ground, we quiz Brayford on his wheels – not exactly the flash motor you'd expect for a footballer who spent time at a Premier League club. Was it down to a passion for old-school cars? Not quite. "Me and the missus watched 'The Italian Job', and I just thought, 'I need one of them bastards.' We got it for a good price and it's gone all over the world that thing, from V Festival to everywhere really. And it's still going strong now."

The perks of being a footballer open up a realm of possibilities to those in the profession. The wages and the excess afternoons off mean players can pursue any hobby they wish, but we're often meeting young Premier League players who live and breathe the game without exploring other avenues. It's perhaps wrong to call them boring, as they've been told to focus on the game their entire career, but still … it's kind of boring. Surely there are only so many computer games they can play and Nando's they can eat?

"It would be a pretty dull life if you just finished work at 1pm and had nothing to do," Brayford

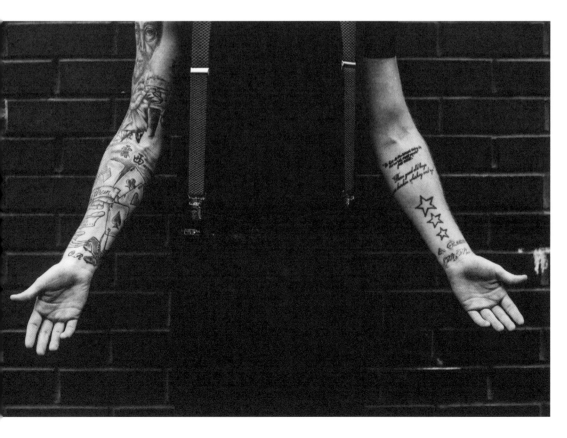

tells us. This comes from a man who visits new cities each year, owns a racehorse, and spent his last couple of summers travelling across America and Germany.

Plying his trade at the oldest professional football ground in the world, Brayford explains his affection for the club as we walk around Bramall Lane. "Most grounds these days are all modernised in out-of-city retail parks, but this is surrounded by little back streets in the heart of the city. There's an old-fashioned feel about it, and I really like that scene."

"When I returned to Cardiff from my loan spell here … it was like there was something missing from my life. It was always in the back of my mind; there was something telling me I had to come back. Cardiff could have gone on and won the Premier League, but if I never came back here I'd have always thought what might have been." Turning down money for the love of a club, having a pint with the fans and having an identity of his own are maverick tendencies for us. A true throwback. Is football still cool? You tell us.

Stylish Football: John Brayford looking typically dapper outside Bramall Lane.

@ilovedust

RED REBELS RISING

—

F.C. United of Manchester

Photography by Robbie Jay Barrett

F.C. United of Manchester is a tale of glorious rebellion. A story of remarkable feats. Old Trafford is a distant memory as Broadhurst Park sees dreams become reality. A theatre in which everyone has a leading role, this feature is dedicated to the memory of Russell Delaney, "who gave the last weeks of his life establishing the football club".

Offering a powerful insight behind the scenes of this maverick club, we caught up with general manager Andy Walsh to get his take on what it means to tear up the rule book and go back to the roots of football. Not short of conviction, the passion is palpable and the spirit is rich. This is football.

"I'll give up my season ticket and I'll stop going to games, but I want to continue the fight from within." As one of the fans who originally opposed the creation of F.C. United of Manchester, Andy is someone that provides a unique perspective.

A Manchester United fan since birth, he was exposed to the excitement of live football from an early age. "I started going to games with my dad before I started going to school. I went to my first away game when I was five. It was Burnley away." It was the power of those that paved the way to Old Trafford who also opened the door to F.C. United. "It was my dad and my son who persuaded me that maybe we should start going to F.C. United."

TED

Having been "involved in the independent Manchester United Supporters Association and successfully campaigned on supporter issues with the club", most notably the prevention of the takeover of Manchester United by Rupert Murdoch, Andy took some persuading to give F.C. United a chance. With so much time put into trying to hold onto the values of the fans that the club established, it was the Glazer takeover that finally acted as the catalyst for him to give up his season ticket. And he wasn't alone.

"Even the board of directors at Manchester United [had concerns]. David Gill famously said it was going to put too much debt on the club, and we still couldn't stop it. Quite a few people had felt disaffected, disenfranchised from the club for a good period of time."

Walking away from a lifetime of support is no easy task, though with positive tunes focusing on strengths over weaknesses, Andy notes a mantra that has helped define what F.C. United now stands for. "It's not enough just to say what you're against, you've got to say what you're in favour of as well – and that's why we created F.C. United."

The fanaticism of those that first led the charge towards creating a break-away club is something that lasts in the memory for Andy. "I was pretty awe-struck by the people involved in the steering committee – they knew far more than me." Having been invited to join the steering committee, it wasn't long before his role took flight, with the free-thinking pioneers' inspired enthusiasm rubbing off quickly. "Just being around these people and listening to what they had done … in just a couple of short weeks they had put so much in place to create F.C. United."

Human beings are extraordinary. Often we look at football and evangelise about just how fantastic a game it is – there's no questioning that. But it would be nothing without those people providing the flair, the energy and the inspired moments. The foundations for F.C. United live in blood, sweat and tears of human beings. Having drawn up a manifesto and outlined their strategy, the group's focus turned to funding. "Over 3,000 people pledged their support one way or the other – from the 50p we received

from young children to the four or five grand that we received from some individuals. We raised over £180,000 in those first couple of months." Having a lump sum of cash on the table meant F.C. United were able to make quick and efficient moves to create the club and apply to the relevant governing bodies. No flash in the pan, very much a statement of intent, built on a ruthless strategy of collaborative might.

Shift on to the start of the 15/16 season and F.C. United now stand proud, an established club with a sparkling new stadium. "It's cost £6.3 million to develop this ground, half of which we've raised ourselves - over £2 million in the community share scheme." If there's one thing that captures the power of this united frontier of enthused instigators, it's Broadhurst Park. A jewel in their youth-yielding crown, the club has already experienced several promotions, leaving them sitting a stone's throw from the football league.

Bricks laid, path embarked, it is here that we can discover more about the cement that binds this club together. Crowd funding on many levels, the innovative use of social investment tax relief schemes has given the members of the club the chance to put in, and quite literally reap what they sow. And they get plenty back – emotionally, visibly and financially. "The community share scheme allows ordinary people like us, and football fans in particular, to raise the sort of finance that in the past has just not been available. The thought that ordinary fans would raise over £2 million for a football ground is unprecedented. But now we've got our scheme, we've got Wrexham, Chester, Portsmouth, Enfield Town – all these clubs are able to raise money through the community share scheme that we helped develop."

A policy of "all out commercialism", the club's strategy can be determined by the fact that they proudly have a main club sponsor but don't have it emblazoned across the front of shirts – something their investors buy into. "We're pushing the boundaries all the time and giving people a real say in a way that can positively affect their lives."

"The focus for us is about whether it's affordable for people to come and watch us. We have to make sure

the club is sustainable and make sure we can pay the players the sort of money that will attract them to stay here. Most of our players aren't paid anything like what other players are paid in our league, but we look after them. They play in a fantastic facility. They've got supporters cheering them on every week, and they haven't got that anywhere else – over 3,000 people. We're something like the 4th or 5th best supported non-league club in the country."

The price of football a constant debate, it's something that F.C. United are trying to balance, with fans the most important commodity. "We've set our gate price as low as we can afford to. Our gate prices are £9 when the average in the league is probably about £12." The club embraces new ideas and contemporary thinking. "We have a 'pay what you can afford' season ticket scheme here where the minimum price is £100. Anything over and above that is a donation. The average price that we get for a season ticket is £148, and we've got more season ticket holders now than we've ever had. We've got over 2,000 season ticket holders."

Growing at a rapid rate, the infectious trail is most certainly blazing above and beyond the world of non-league football. The professional game echoes down the corridors of Broadhurst Park. "We set a target of 2,700 average gate here – we're over 3,400." It's a similar story for contributing members, as a goal of 4,500 was reached and surpassed within a single month. F.C. United is now on course to become "the biggest member-owned football club in the country."

Breaking into new ground for the beautiful game, F.C. are in every sense United. "We're taking it in a slightly different direction. Taking it back to many of its core values. It's about participation, about physical activity, about community and bringing people together." Armed with flags, spirit and free-thinking vibrancy, it's an almighty mission, a success story that continues to unfold. Built by the fans, for the fans, memories are being created on a daily basis and spreading into the local community triumphantly. It's time to get involved in your club.

Right Andy Walsh, General Manager of F.C. United. Immensly proud of the combined effort that has produced the club.

Above Flags grace all areas of Broadhurst Park, the crowdfunded home of F.C. United. A remarkable achievement dressed from seam to seam in united passions.

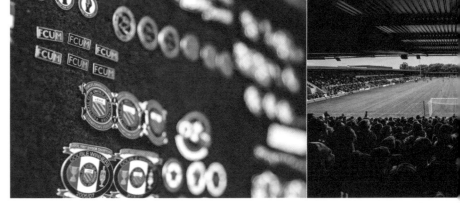

Above From pin badges to punk football. The wooden clad exterior symbolic of railway sleepers. A nod to Newton Heath.

Left Not short of support. Fans of all ages have taken to Broadhurst Park. Players united, shirts do not contain the name of a primary sponsor. Independent football for the masses.

Middle Groundsman Graham Byrne looks on ahead of kick off. Pitch immaculate, it's a beautiful place to both watch and play.

SWAZZY

—

Jay Emmanuel-Thomas

Photography by James Hendley

Sat in a Finsbury Park barbers with one of QPR's summer additions, we're in to get a trim off the sides as Jay Emmanuel-Thomas talks us through his career to date. Unorthodox in his own right and a 6ft 3in game-changer, he's a player of instinctive qualities.

From Arsenal to QPR via Ipswich Town and Bristol City, not to mention opportunities to learn while out on loan at Blackpool, Doncaster Rovers and Cardiff City, the man known as JET is a presence of energy. A humble spark, he invites us in to share an afternoon and get a glimpse of his world. Dumbfounding defenders, tricking midfielders and out-calming keepers, it's not a dull one.

Emmanuel-Thomas is a character, a player with personality and one that positively doesn't fit the prototypical mould of a striker. "I'm 6ft 3 but I like running with the ball. It's not really a combination that comes about that often. Most players my size tend to play more as a target man or a centre half, or in midfield, so I couldn't compare myself to another player."

Very much a creator as much as he is a finisher, Emmanuel-Thomas began his career at Arsenal as a youth player until reaching the fringes of the first team and making his debut against Chelsea. It is something he reflects on with fond memories. "When I made my debut for Arsenal it was against Chelsea, so at the time you had that whole solid back line of Ivanovic, Terry, Alex and Ashley Cole. The challenge there is who to go towards; it's hard to pick out who is the weakest link because there isn't really one in that back line. That Chelsea team was unreal."

Appreciative of the education he achieved at The Gunners, a few hair styles down the line he explains, "I've got a soft spot for Arsenal [because] I spent so many years there. They gave me the base of my career. They taught me the style of football that I play now, which is never going to leave." Now part of a QPR squad mounting a campaign to return to the top flight of English football, Arsenal is now very much in the past for Emmanuel-Thomas as he settles into life at Loftus Road.

Celebrating his intuitive on-pitch methodology, it has been all about finding the right match for Emmanuel-Thomas. He left the West Country on good terms after enjoying a strong couple of years at Bristol City, becoming a fan favourite and a title and cup winner in the process. "Bristol City fans showed me a lot of love and same for the Ipswich fans. Maybe it's just because of the way I play; I like to think there's a lot of excitement in my game." Scoring 33 goals for Bristol City including a thunderbolt against rivals Rovers, it's no surprise QPR came calling. For the player, it was about putting the jigsaw together – something often a lot easier said than done, especially when you don't fit the mould of convention. "Because of the style in which I play, a lot depends on the manager I'm playing under. If you find the right manager and the right club, it always becomes a lot easier and that's when you can really work towards going in the right direction."

Short back and #SWAZZY. JET takes it all
in his stride, professionally sharp.

Shout out to @Tstyles_ for letting us in
for the afternoon.

"It doesn't have a proper meaning; it's just a phrase for when something is big. Instead of excellent, it's SWAZZY."

—

That direction is an upward trajectory, which saw him settle in the capital, and Emmanuel-Thomas clearly has the head and determination to take his chances when they come. It's at this point that the mini Segways start gliding about this grown-up playground of good vibes – in its own way a Tamagotchi for post-teenage players – and it's a demonstration of his natural ability as he steps on for the first time and gets it instantly. Balance isn't an issue. A smile beaming, that's where the deeper character starts to come through.

As a professional athlete, fun is as much a part of his game as anything else. And he's as interesting off the pitch as he is on it. Lethal Bizzle and Chipmunk are both musicians he calls good friends among a scene that shapes a big part of his life. Appearing in a few music videos along the way, he's also inked-up with pride, having accumulated the best part of 50 hours under the needle. His proudest tattoo represents the name of his daughter and sits below his shoulders underneath the words 'Emmanuel-Thomas', which stretches the width of his back. "They've mainly been done in Finchley by a tattoo artist called Rakhee Shah." His appreciation for creativity goes back to his school days. "There was a girl at my school who did my most recent one, Jade Chanel Pereira. She was always drawing. I've always been a fan of her art. I used to find myself just sitting there and looking at her work. She's seriously talented."

Equally, there is a level of focus on the pitch that Emmanuel-Thomas champions, a quality of the predatory nature of strikers that cuts him apart. He relishes the challenge ahead as he notes, "I would like to play against Hazard or Alexis Sanchez because they are the type of player that on their day are probably unplayable." Unfazed by the stage that the game presents, especially at Loftus Road where the crowd is so close to the players, his confidence in his own ability is where he lays out the task in hand. "Sometimes you have to try and block it out and ignore the atmosphere as that can swing your performance. If you do something wrong, and start listening to what people are saying, [then] some players can get put off by that. Not all, but some. So I guess you've just got to try and blank it out and let go as soon as you cross the white line and focus on the game." Often capitalising on those players in the opposition he identifies as weak links, his observations are acute. "You can tell those situations where you know a player should do something with the ball or play in a type of way, but they don't and they won't take the risk because if they do, the fans might get on to them and their head might go. It's one of those things where it's so important that everyone knows their role in the team."

JET is a guy of perspective. Rather than get caught up on the often oh-so-serious side of football, he keeps his feet firmly on the ground. In brand new Jordan sneakers, we might add. Humble in his approach, his take on swapping shirts pretty much sums him up. "I like to get them from people I've played with in the past. They mean a little more. I take pride in what each of them is doing." Equally, his coined phrase of 'SWAZZY' adds weight to the personality of this light-hearted on-and-off-the-pitch entertainer. "It doesn't have a proper meaning; it's just a phrase for when something is big. Instead of excellent, it's SWAZZY. Every tweet I get has #SWAZZY at the end. I told fans if you don't have #SWAZZY at the end then I won't reply."

STILL BUZZING

—

Christian Stadil

Photography by Jon Roberts

If ever a brand's image was replicated by its owner's personality then it's Hummel. Christian Stadil is an entrepreneur with eggs in many baskets, but his largest is decorated with two big old chevrons.

Hummel was born in 1923, making it one of the oldest sports brands in the world, with an imperative focus on football from the very start. The brand has been responsible for some of the most revolutionary products, including the first screw-in studded football boot – a moment that flamboyant owner Christian Stadil talks us through.

Christian is one of a kind. He's led the Hummel charge since 1999 and has reignited the brand through a combination of charisma, determination, and a pinch of crazy. The word Hummel comes from the German word for bumblebee, as Christian explains. "As the story goes, a shoemaker was watching a football match and the players couldn't stand because of the rain, so that inspired him to find a new way of working with studded cleats. The players could then dribble better, pull off flicks, and make changes of direction that they shouldn't have been able to do. As with the bumblebee, which shouldn't be able to carry its own weight."

Hummel were the first brand to use exclusive designs on jerseys and aimed to work differently to change the overall look of football shirts. The brand's drive and diversity installed Hummel as one of the biggest football brands in Europe throughout the 1980's – at one point they sponsored Benfica, Udinese, Spurs, Aston Villa, and Real Madrid. Hummel were serious players, and it was that history and potential that inspired Christian to buy the company in 1999.

Football has changed considerably since those days. Some changes indisputably for the better, but some for the worse. The game is becoming more business-orientated, as Christian explains. "The reason we could get so many sponsorships was because football wasn't so money driven as it is today. Today it's about the size of your wallet; back then it was about respect and relationships."

"We sponsored the Danish national team for 20 years. The golden days for Hummel with Denmark came in 1992 when they were a wildcard to the European Championships and ended up winning the

"The reason we could get so many
sponsorships was because football
wasn't so money driven as it is today.
Today it's about the size of your wallet,
back then it was about respect
and relationships."

tournament, beating Germany in the final - that was a big moment for us but the company went bankrupt just two years later. We had a super-cheap contract with the national team and jersey sales went through the roof but it wasn't enough to save the company."

Hummel would have been buried in the football graveyard had it not been for Christian, who successfully reconstructed the brand when he took over before the turn of the millennium. The company needed fresh blood, new ideas and an injection of enthusiasm, something Christian has an infectious abundance of. "We looked at how we could rebrand Hummel, and one of the things we did was to reintroduce the brand into the marketplace as a fashion label. We were one of the first sports brands to do this, taking original sports style from the 70's and 80's. I had a good network in music and film, so I went around the world, doing about 65,000 km a year, trying to sell Hummel and to get all these people to wear it. Eventually I got a lot of the best shops in the world on board."

"We closed the door and partied all night and all the models just took pictures of each other."

Denmark is the only nation in the world that has a sports brand bigger than adidas and Nike, and that success has allowed Christian to grow other markets. To challenge with the heavyweights in the sports industry you have to think differently or get knocked-out. "We have to think outside the box with marketing compared to other brands" he tells us. A prime example of Christian's free-thinking was when he took 10 models, 100 instant cameras, 10 bottles of booze and a boom-blaster, and placed them in the Royal Hotel suite in Copenhagen for a 1960's style party.

"We closed the door and partied all night – all the models just took pictures of each other. Behind the curtain was the whole Hummel collection, which they could just take off and put on. In the morning, when the party was over, some of the pictures looked like shit because they were drunk, but some of them had a powerful raw feel to them, and we made a catalogue that only cost about £5,000. It went around the world and we won awards for it." Christian is in it for the good times. Work hard, party harder.

Hummel are small in comparison to adidas and Nike, so for Christian it's about doing things that those monsters can't do. Decisions for multi-million pound campaigns need to be signed off a hundred times and can take years to plan, but if Christian wants to do something, he'll do it. He's the sole owner. Simple.

"Who owns adidas and Nike? I don't know. They have so many stockholders from all over the world. We have one stockholder: me. That allows us to do stuff that other brands can't. They can have sensors under the pitch to test stud pressure – we can't afford that, but we can do something else."

"We were put on this earth to change the world of sports. That's what we live for, that's what is most important to us," Christian proudly states. Hummel are a brand of ethics and will only collaborate with partners that share their vision and fit their way of doing things.

The brand's image is incredibly important for Christian, and he likes to think that there's a certain kind of person that is attracted to Hummel. "We don't want to hire assholes. Hummel is like a family and we don't take ourselves too seriously. All my colleagues can call me or drop me a text; we don't have a strict hierarchy, we have an open doors policy."

Hummel are now a successful sports fashion brand thanks to the resurgence led by Christian, and what makes the story all the more impressive is the amount of other plates Christian is spinning whilst running the company. "In the last two years I've invested in or co-founded over 20 different companies." One of those projects is tattoodo.com, the world's biggest tattoo community with over 22 million unique visitors a month. "I co-founded that with a group of people, including Daniel Agger. But out of all the companies I'm involved with, Hummel has the most potential, because if we take just 3% market share from Nike and 5% market share from adidas, then we'd be a huge company."

Christian flourishes in the position of Hummel being the underdog and lists a simple combination of objectives for the brand's future. "We want to combine making money with making a difference. In the next 10 years are we going to be as big as Nike and adidas? No. But we can be in the same revenue realm as the likes of PUMA and Under Armour."

"We like doing things that have an intellectual edge to them, that's where we want to be." With Christian Stadil at the helm, Hummel will always be distinctively edgy.

Half Way Line

Pass + Move
Pass + M

He's done it!!

BAR KICK

–

A Continental Tipple

Photography by James Hendley

As we gather round as spectators to many a football scene, the amphitheatre of choice is a crucial one when not sitting in the stands. Forever on a quest to discover the greatest places to watch many a battle, we head to Bar Kick in Shoreditch to take in a celebration of football culture.

Bar Kick sits proudly at the end of Shoreditch High Street. Decorated top-to-toe in an eclectic mix of football memorabilia from all over the world, every day is a match day of refreshing proportions. From table football to Champions League finals, its unpretentious appreciation of football is explained by manager Gareth Kerr.

As an established and well-lived resident of Shoreditch, can you give us an introduction into the history of Bar Kick?
Bar Kick came to life in 2001 after we stumbled across this old shoe shop in Shoreditch. On a very, very small budget, we put together a very bare and plain bar – all we could afford – and luckily from night one we were blessed with beautiful customers!

Match days are special – what do you think makes them so unique?
We used to use this very cheesy description: 'Where the world meets and smiles'. We have always aimed

Right Every day is a matchday. Atmosphere vocal and on point. Don your kit.

194

to make our spirit free, with a real wish to please everyone, but [it's] probably best judged by coming along. I think if you appreciate football for football you will very much feel at home in our bar.

We had this regular, Steve, who unfortunately is no longer with us. He was a mad season-ticket holding football lover: he once shouted at me, maybe a little worse for wear, across a very busy Bar Kick, "This is the best bloody place to watch football outside the stadium!" And, probably equally worse for wear, I agreed with him.

There are tons of stories on the walls, all sorts of memorabilia. Where have you collected it from over the years?

Everything we have – or most things – at both Cafe Kick and Bar Kick has come from our customers. They bring us scarves, local currency, flags, pictures – all sorts of stuff. Once we had this guy walk in who had just used this life sized copy of a table football player he had made for a Lion Bar commercial and gave it to us. We are very lucky.

What are your greatest football memories at the bar? Are there any games that stand out more than most?

One memory is [from] when I was not even there. It was Arsenal v Barcelona in the 2006 final, the bar was as busy as it gets and I was in hospital waiting for the

birth of my first boy. And when he was born, halfway through the second half, the bar went nuts. But to be honest I have watched so much football in Kick [that] there are too many memories to remember.

What about future plans? You already have the cafe, are there any plans afoot to venture to any other parts of London, the UK or indeed the world?
We have plans to open another bar in London very soon, and all being well hopefully we will be looking in other cities around the UK. Beyond that would be one in New York – we can dream!

What can people expect as a place to watch the European Championships in the summer of 2016?
People can expect us to be a bloody great place to watch the tournament. Over time we have built up such good experience in the big footballing occasions. And we look forward to welcoming everyone.

From the welcome invite of shared decoration by its customers to the widespread flavour of many nationalities, Bar Kick demonstrates the power of football in bringing likeminded people together. Whatever nationality or team supported, the bar has the power to feel personal to each individual while resonating as a place of the people – open to all. Table football awaits, no spinning.

Above Memorabilia mounting. A feast on the eyes, charming on the tastebuds. A banquet of cultured proportions.

Right Alfresco football. The spill of regulars out onto the streets, it gets busy. Brilliantly so.

EN
PROBLÈME ?

–

Samir Nasri

Photography by Jon Roberts

Say what you want about Samir Nasri. Question his motives, his decisions, his attitude but not his individuality or his thirst for success. Not that he cares what you think anyway.

"If I'm not happy about something I'm going to tell you, for example if this interview doesn't go well I will tell you, it's just the way I am."

—

Modern football can be very black and white and clubs have increased efforts to control their players in order to protect their assets. Perhaps wisely, players are granted limited media access and drip-fed scripts when they are allowed in front of the camera. As a result, it makes players cautious and forces them to offer only what fans want to hear, and what the media expects to hear.

Samir Nasri doesn't read scripts, though; he writes them.

"If I'm not happy about something I'm going to tell you. For example, if this interview doesn't go well I will tell you. It's just the way I am." Gulp. It's difficult to gauge whether he's joking but the longer we talk it becomes apparent that he's a man true to his word. He has an endearing take-it-or-leave-it personality and it seems he's not likely to change. Mavericks come in many forms and Samir Nasri's route into this issue is his honesty – a unique trait in a game that is littered with smoke and mirrors.

Sweep off the sugar-coated finish and elite level football is a tough industry that can eat up players and spit them out quicker than academies can produce them. The very best players need a tough exterior with confidence and a winning attitude backed up by talent, and Nasri has all of those attributes combined with an opinionated mind that makes him a rarity in the game.

Samir was born and raised in the hard-working community of Marseille, France and this is where his gritty, no bullshit, take no prisoners attitude comes from. "Where you were brought up and who you grew up with is what defines your personality [and] I'm really proud of what I've become. I'm a guy who is honest and I expect people to be the same way with me. Yeah, that sometimes causes me problems, but I'm OK about that. People know where they stand when they are around me."

Marseille is responsible for producing two of the most maverick of players to ever play the game; two legends in Zinedine Zidane and Eric Cantona; two players who were role models to Samir when he was growing up. Not just because of their eloquent playing style but because of their controversial traits and outspoken mannerisms. It made them exciting and when they spoke, you listened. "It was good looking up to those players, who were also from Marseille and huge characters, but at the same time

it was difficult because at a really young age I was compared to Zidane, so there was a lot of weight on my shoulders."

Cantona especially was a player that, like Nasri, had his own mind and wasn't fazed about discussing matters when other players would shy away. He upset his fair share of managers, journalists and one particularly outspoken Crystal Palace fan along the way, but Nasri admits that whole unpredictable nature of Cantona's personality made him even more intriguing. "Do I see some of his personality in myself? Yeah, but I think he was a little bit worse than me. He was on another level. I say things but I'm not going to Kung-Fu kick a fan in the face!" Fair enough, good to know that's where he draws the line. "He's a really special character, though, and he was a special player, too. He would do things on the pitch that other players would never try to do and simply couldn't do. That was just the way he was. For me he was an artist, he was crazy, but I loved the guy. That type of character is fascinating."

"I love those types of players. I love players who have a big mouth but they deliver on the pitch. Nowadays that would be Zlatan. He'll talk but he will always deliver on the pitch [and] if you're just all talk but don't perform on the pitch you're not credible. All the best players are confident – a little bit crazy, but confident."

Samir's move from Arsenal to Manchester City demonstrates how the world of football is completely different to any other industry. If you were offered a huge pay rise to do the same job, aside from numerous promotion and trophy opportunities, you'd take it. It's a no brainer, especially if you knew you had to end your career in your early thirties. Most intelligent football fans would accept that, but football can be a fickle business and quite often

supporters' passion and loyalty to their own clubs can blur their vision towards a player's decisions; a hero at one club will always be a villain at another. "You can try to be the perfect player but you can never be perfect. People are always going to hate you because that's just the way it is, so play your own way and don't worry about pleasing everyone [because] that's impossible. The gap between the players and the fans isn't helped by a lot of talk about money in the papers, so when you don't deliver on the pitch fans will always criticise you. They'll say he's on 100k or 200k a week so players want to protect themselves. They're not going to be that close to the fans. The relationship between them has changed a little bit and that's sad because we are where we are because of the fans and we should have a good relationship."

Social media has allowed players to let fans into their selective lifestyles, which goes some way to bridging the gap in the relationship, while at the same time offering a platform for fans to directly interact with the players, although not always in a civilised manner as we've all seen. So is Samir bothered by torrents of abuse from the terraces and keyboard warriors? In hindsight, that was a stupid question. "Seriously? I do not care." Told you. "I don't know any player that every single fan in the world loves. When I see comments on Twitter or on Instagram when I post a picture, I just laugh at it. Seriously, it's not going to change my life that you say I'm this or that. It makes me laugh, I look at it with my friends and team-mates and we all laugh at them."

Samir is 28 now and his football education has taught him to trust a select few people, which everyone can relate to. But while his personality can come across as dismissive and obnoxious (it feels as if we're always one question away from pissing him off), he's aware of that and it's for good reason. "I'm not an open person. If I don't know you I can be rude and stuff

but it's just a cover and a way of protecting myself. I only open up to my close friends and my family. It's important to protect yourself."

Football can be simplified when it comes to a player's mindset and that goes from grass roots right the way through to the very top. "I'm like every player. If I'm playing I'm good fun, if I don't play then I'm moody. Simple. Ask my managers; some will say I'm nice, some will say I'm difficult to deal with on a daily basis, but that normally depends if I'm in the team."

Nasri's maverick mentality is inspired by his vision to create new history rather than adding to something that already exists, and that played an important role

> "Ask my managers, some will say I'm nice, some will say I'm difficult to deal with."

in him joining New Balance. "I was with adidas for ten years but I needed a change and this was the best opportunity. It's like what I did with Manchester City; I had Manchester United wanting to sign me but I went for City because I wanted to be part of history. I wanted to be a proper member of it, and when I spoke with New Balance there were a lot of similarities. We have the same approach and we want to do the same things, so it was an easy decision."

Individuality and feedback from only the people who matter are what is valuable to Samir, but that wasn't always the case. He grew up like many of us, hungry for positive feedback and eager for recognition. "When I was younger I used to read the newspaper after every game to see what they'd say about me and it affected me. If the journalist said that I didn't play well I would have some doubt going into the next game, so I told myself that's not going to change anything and I began not caring what they would say. I just started working for myself and I don't read newspapers now. I don't care what they have to say."

Under his bulletproof exterior and unique personality, Nasri still shares one common love with all his colleagues and opposition – football. We all grow up obsessed with the game as kids and that love affair can drift away with age, but that's not the case for Nasri. He's tough and intelligent and somewhat intimidating but with a ball at his feet he's happy. "I still love the game, I still respect the game. If I could start again I would not be that naïve at the start of my career and assume that everyone was nice and everyone wants what is best for you. That's not how it is. You have to be a team player but at the same time you need to be selfish and look at what is actually best for you. I love the game and I'm playing in the best league in the world. It's the best thing that ever happened in my life and for this I will always love it."

Samir Nasri wears the
New Balance Visaro.

CROSS
THE
LINE

ROBBiE

@lawerta

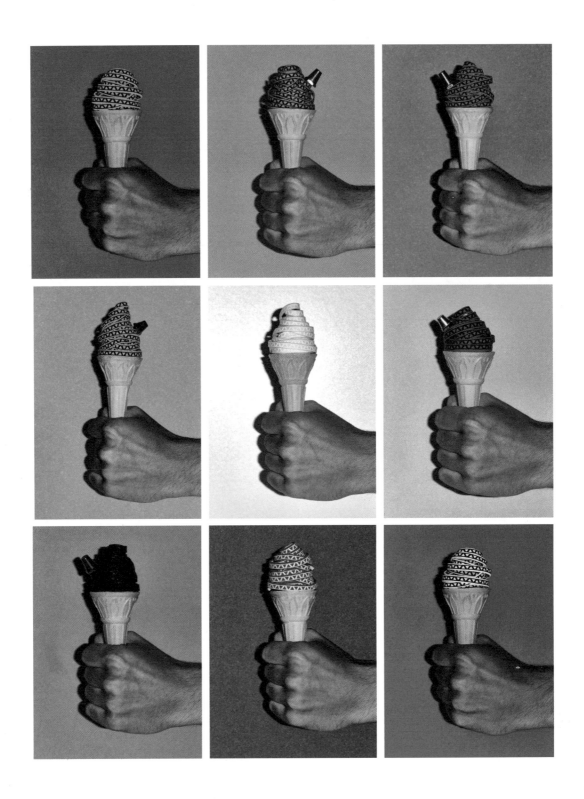

AMO

—

What's your flavour? AMO is the new sweet shop of football customisation, a pick 'n mix parlour that enables players to add a personalised touch to their boots in the form of coloured laces and studs. A visual upgrade with a competitive edge - the waterproof polyester Grip Lace has a textured silicon coating that enhances ball touch and minimises lace slip. Two scoops please.